WHERE GROWN MEN CRY

Manufactured in the United States of America

FIRST EDITION

Cormac, Inc.
P. O. Box 62808
Washington, D. C. 20029

Library of Congress Cataloging in Publication Data
Slaughter, James N. Jr., 1927–
    Where grown men cry.

    1. Church work with prisoners. I. Jackson, David James. II. Title.
BV4340.S53   1986   255'.5   86–32665
ISBN 0–9617749–0–8

The purpose of this book is to enlighten the reader on the effects of an endeavor to replenish spirituality often lost by inmates as a result of incarceration. It is not intended to justify criminal acts resulting in incarceration.

ISBN 0–9617749–0–8

Cover and illustrations by James N. Slaughter, Jr.,

Photographs by John Bechet and Nathaniel Brooks

WHERE GROWN MEN CRY

An endeavor to free the spirit in a prison.

A detailed description of a prison project

by
James N. Slaughter, Jr.

Edited by: David James Jackson

BookCrafters/Chelsea, Michigan
Cormac, Inc.   *1986*

Dedication

As my wife desires, this book is dedicated
to our little grandson,
Gerard A. Blackshear, Jr.,

to

David James Jackson, Pastor of the Randall Memorial
United Methodist Church, Washington, District of
Columbia, for his significant contribution. Without his
continued, sustaining support, untiring efforts,
tolerance and assistance, this manuscript would not
have been possible;

and to

prison volunteers and ministries it may inspire.

Epigraph

I spend my time in prison wondering about the future. Surroundings will not permit needed concentration. Forever plagued, when do I go wherever I'm going? What do I do for a future if I get there?

—An Inmate

WHERE GROWN MEN CRY

An endeavor to free the spirit

Table of Contents

Preface

This manuscript, titled "WHERE GROWN MEN CRY", may be considered a response to several situations. Numbered among the situations is a particular prison compound where more than a thousand men survive from day to day in a seemingly deprived, impersonal, dehumanizing and spiritually deficient environment.

Situation number two is the effort of my wife, Bernice, a diminutive woman recovering from the effects of a massive heart attack, motivated to use her special talents to help the prisoners within that prison compound. In the process she has helped herself and inspired other volunteers to serve in a place where "angels" fear to tread.

The third situation is my own deep-seated feeling that much needed to be done to help fellow human beings in penal institutions.

Situation number four is that an extremely disproportionate number of Black men, nearly 100%, were confined within the barbed-wire fences of a particular institution.

Initially, mine was an apprehension for the safety of Bernice when she mentioned forming an inmates' choir. There was even concern for my own safety while contemplating a visit to the institution. This fear was lessened when she returned safely from a visit and reported the respectful manner in which the prisoners treated her. Upon my arrival, my approach to individual inmates appeared to lessen the distance between us.

During several visits when Bernice played songs and all of us sang in enthusiastic fellowship, suspicions and apprehensions melted away. Added to this was the chapel renovation project which helped to further dispel any residual distrust that the residents might have had about volunteers. Converging occurrences often produce interesting effects. The spirited responses of the residents to the newly-formed choir, to the renovation efforts and to the landscaping brought increased expressions of appreciation. These expressions often were accompanied by handshakes, embraces, verbal and written messages. Consequently, a considerable number of men voiced desires to alter their lifestyles. And, they did.

It was encouraging to feel the more relaxed atmosphere. The concern shown the prisoners and their increased participation apparently were producing the intended results. As I observed an improving situation, I became more hopeful for those isolated, depressed, unstimulated and non-achieving human beings. Their potential for fulfilled lives became increasingly less stymied. The distress I felt over their plight caused me to seek relief for them and for myself. I informed the community of the situation—the travesty discovered upon my wife's arrival, and the incredible rejuvenation witnessed since her involvement.

The community must know why its active involvement is required to influence prison reform. The combination of circumstances, observations and feelings occasioned the conclusion that this book must be published.

Foreword

One vision did lead to the formation of a community-supported project of critical magnitude. The accomplishment helped to form a bridge between the penal institution and the community. Consequently, the community became privy to a more in-depth introduction to the institution. The experience had both rewarding and disconcerting effects. It is noteworthy, the measure of benefit derived from it by the inmates. Ironically, there is no shortage of evidence that the quality of administration by the District of Columbia Department of Corrections may well have contributory culpability for the problems of recidivism, as well as inmate disaffection.

It is a noble task which was attempted and achieved. It was an approach to the task of ministry in prison that is, at least, unique and possibly without parallel. Can there be another volunteer anywhere like this one? Where is it likely to be discovered on this planet a kind and quality of commitment to prison residents and their well-being, of comparable scope? Is it not so that prisons everywhere would be the better as a consequence? And what if there were no few such volunteers, those of genuine and high interest? Oh, what an impressive scenario that reality would foster. And ultimately, would there not be a different kind of prison life for the inmate? What great potential, then, for a vastly different kind of community reception for the newly released ex-offender, returning to society. Might it not be that the prevailing propensity toward nearly certain re-imprisonment could be altered in a fashion of no little consequence?

Seemingly, a prison system populated by administrators and correctional workers—in large numbers—visibly demonstrating real interest in inmate well-being, would have caused desirable effects. A systematic attempt at reconstructing the lives of prisoners undoubtedly would have lessened the difficulty attendant to this volunteer effort. Administrative cooperation and support, demonstratively actualized, as opposed to deceptively feigned, ought to have diminished the obstacles, the barriers, the inordinate difficulties and unconscionable frustration needlessly thrown up against this one's selfless offering of her own time, energy, and human and financial resources. Is this to be construed as the norm within correctional institutions across the country; or, may it be considered that such hostile administrative resistance and conniving dishonesty is peculiar to a minority of prison systems? Against a backdrop such as this, is there any wonder that recidivism is so prominently positioned among the lengthy listing of prison concerns? This volume does offer a rather startling introduction to a system presumed to be unnecessarily vile, inconceivably venomous. It does explore the consequential impact upon the ones over whom the system has jurisdiction, as well as the ones who dare to volunteer themselves in service. Forthrightly does it approach the varied issues, concerns and realities of the whole matter. It is exemplary in its depiction of determined, persistent effort to help the captive, in the face of the jail-keeper's alleged vindictive resentment. So that, it is informational, it ought to be motivational; and, it is intended to be instructional.

David James Jackson
Chairman, Board of Directors
EVOL Prison Ministry, Inc.,
Washington, D. C.

Introduction

This book tells the story of a talented, determined and resourceful woman who would not take *no* for an answer as she persevered to form an inmates' choir at Occoquan Prison, spearheaded a drive to renovate the Occoquan Chapel, and created a spiritual enrichment program there. This effort was further buttressed by a sponsorship program for inmates.

Occoquan I and II is one of eight institutions of the District of Columbia Department of Corrections, located within 3,000 acres of land in Fairfax County, Virginia. The population of Occoquan I and II is approximately 1,300 inmates. This book reveals the experiences of the mission of an exuberant religious volunteer at Occoquan I and II.

Bernice Brent Slaughter, a deceptively small package, housing an immense spirit and drive, single-handedly encouraged, inspired, guided, and directed the formation of the choir, creation of the spiritual program and major renovation of the chapel.

Despite coming back virtually from the grave after a major heart attack nearly fourteen years ago, and despite having to leave a tension-filled job on Capitol Hill as a result of her illness, Bernice decided to become a volunteer choir organizer at Occoquan, a D. C. prison facility in Virginia. After beginning her mission, she saw that the Occoquan residents' needs were greater than she had ever imagined. She immediately started seeking funds from all corners of the community to defray the cost of the renovation and programs.

Ministers, churches, church conferences, private individuals and companies donated approximately $40,000 over a five-month period for the most costly aspect of the project—the chapel renovation. Part of the estimated value consisted of in-kind contributions.

Occoquan *residents supplied the labor* to renovate the chapel and landscape its grounds, an effort that had monetary as well as personal benefits for the residents. They saved the costs of what a commercial company would have charged to renovate a chapel now estimated to have a *$150,000 market value.*

More importantly, for the modest outlay of sweat and effort, the residents reaped the incalculable benefit of *raising their self-esteem* because of the tangible effort (renovating the chapel) they made to better their lives.

Bernice's story details the five months it took to complete the chapel renovation and, how men of various faiths set aside their differences to realize a common goal. This story serves as a reminder that *will* can triumph over many seemingly insurmountable obstacles. Perhaps the most formidable obstacle was the intimidation of ministers by some of the staff.

Radio, television, magazines, newspapers, and many citizens have recognized this project as an exceptional example of how the community can coalesce behind one woman's vision and make that vision a living reality for positive change.

Acknowledgments

In various ways, many have made significant contributions in the preparation of the manuscript. To them, I offer my thanks—Evelyn Arrington, James Bronson, Jr., Larry Collins, Jaronza Ellis, Barbara Graham, Sandra Lumpkin, Bridgett Lacey, Eve Nightengale, Joseph Parker, Ted Peters, Thomasina Smith, Georgie Thomas and Nathaniel Thomas.

For his guidance, support and inspiration from abroad, a special thanks to Harcourt Bastian, Nassau, Bahamas and to Janelle Brown and Dr. Willie McCloud.

Helping to surmount many obstacles, I salute the EVOL Prison Ministry, Inc.,—Janis Allen, Barbara Bowen, LaVerne Dickerson, Consuelo and Edward Gantt, Juanita Griffin, Mazie Sellers, Alice Young, and Pastors Earl Day, Sr., Archie Griffin, David James Jackson, Robert E. Owens, Arthur A. Preston and Herbert A. Schwandt.

For his sensitivity to my wife's desire to help somebody, and for his close and frequent monitoring of her health—a special thanks to her cardiologist, Dr. Tazewell Banks who consented to her volunteer endeavor.

To the staff employees, officers and some representatives of the system for their concern, interest, assistance and their attempts to override the opposition to this Spiritual effort, I am extremely grateful. It is for obvious reasons names have been omitted.

Special thanks to Daniel Fleming and other legal advisors who reviewed the manuscript and cordially shared their insights.

In any undertaking, there are unsung heroes. To my family and many friends for their patience, forbearance and unceasing support, I remain forever appreciative.

CHAPTER I

Road to Occoquan

The jangling of the telephone grated on Bernice's frazzled nerves and interrupted her concentration as her fingers flew over her typewriter keyboard. "Hello, Senator's office," she replied as her gaze flitted over the piles of papers on her desk. Out of the corner of her eye Bernice noticed the green light flash on, signaling that her boss was just now striding into the Senate Chamber for an important hearing. Her mind churned as she tried to make sense out of the caller's words, which seemed to pour out of the telephone receiver at her ear.

Almost imperceptibly at first, the familiar sights of the office began to rotate. The report she had been pounding out on the typewriter took on a distinct fuzziness. The clock on the wall began melting into an indistinct blob—not unlike the watches she had seen in Dali's painting. The quiet hum of the electric typewriter took on a peculiar sound—sometimes surging into an annoying roar then just as quickly lapsing into an almost imperceptible drone. What had the caller just said? "What was that?" Bernice asked.

Why was her body behaving in such a strange manner? Had the long hours finally gotten to her mind? Had the pressures of working in the Senate finally affected her emotions? Bernice blinked her eyes, but it did no good. Beads of sweat began forming on her forehead, yet a chill brought goose bumps on her arms. Her stomach started feeling as though it were in mutiny. And an annoying sensation scurried up and down her left arm.

Confused, Bernice knew she had to cut short the conversation. Her mind and body just were not coordinating properly. "Let me call you back," she suggested and dropped the handset into its cradle. Perhaps if she could get to the rest room adjoining the office she could splash a little cold water onto her face. She rose unsteadily from the swivel chair behind her desk. Stumbling from her chair, Bernice reeled toward the powder room. What an observer might think, she didn't know, but it felt to her as though she could move only in slow motion. The room began twisting and turning. The ceiling didn't want to stay in place over head. The level floor suddenly took on a steep slant. The door to the rest room was coming up on the left, but it seemed to be bobbing about. Bernice flung out her arm, managed to push open the door, staggered into the rest room, and collapsed in a heap onto the floor. Only her feet were visible from the rest room door. The cool floor tiles did little to help her regain consciousness, yet somehow she could still hear as a co-worker breezed into the office and saw her lying on the floor.

One look told a young legislative intern that Bernice was seriously ill. "Heart attack!" she screamed as she ran to the phone to summon help. Her diagnosis was correct. Bernice was the third victim of a heart attack on that wing within the past few weeks.

Within minutes the sound of pounding, racing feet reached Bernice's semi-comatose brain. Quickly the Capitol physician surveyed the situation and began administering CPR to the stricken woman. In the meantime the ambulance crew arrived on the scene. Bernice, normally full of energy and sparkling wit, lay weak and unresponsive. Strong hands carefully lifted her onto a stretcher and wheeled her down the hall, into the elevator, down to the first floor, and into the emergency vehicle parked nearby.

Lying motionless in the speeding ambulance, Bernice could hear the wailing of the siren as the vehicle careened southwest on Constitution Avenue, onto Pennsylvania Avenue, passing the White House as it wound its way to the George Washington Hospital. The oxygen mask clamped over her nose and mouth felt awkward, and Bernice tried to shake her head from side to side to fling it off, but it stayed tenaciously in place. Her mind remained active even though her normally energetic body lay there inert. In her mind's eye she could see her mother standing there with her. "I want to thank my mother for helping me raise my own daughters. I want to bid farewell to the world because I just know I will be forever useless," Bernice said to herself as the ambulance turned another corner, jarring her as she lay immobile on the stretcher.

Bernice could also hear the ambulance driver's taut voice as he radioed ahead to the emergency room. "*Possible DOA*" he barked into the microphone. "*DOA?*" Bernice mulled those letters over in her mind. "*Am I dead?*" she wondered. The tires squealed and the siren moaned one last time as the ambulance swung into the driveway leading to the emergency room entrance.

The paramedics leaped from the vehicle as nurses and a physician rushed toward the patient. Inside, more people in white coats dashed about as they hooked the thirty-eight year old, single mother to one machine after another. Within minutes Bernice looked more like a robot than a human being. Deftly an attendant plunged a tube down Bernice's nose while another jabbed an IV needle into a vein. And all the while Bernice could hear beep-beep-beep in the background as an irregular wavy green line flickered across the cathode ray tube of the heart monitor.

Only after about twelve hours did the heroic efforts of a battery of doctors finally pay off as Bernice's heartbeat gradually stabilized.

The next morning when Bernice's eyes fluttered open and she weakly turned her head to take in her surroundings, she spied a bouquet of flowers from the Senate staff. She had worked on the Senator's staff now for over a year. Bernice first met the Senator by way of his capable legislative assistant who selected her from among other candidates. When he had invited her to join the staff, Bernice had been ecstatic. As time passed, she learned of the importance of coping with enormous pressures in a political setting.

Becoming more lucid, Bernice began considering the practical aspects of her new circumstances. Many questions occurred to her: Now what would become of her job? How long would she be laid up? When would she be strong enough to take up her duties once again? And would there even be a job waiting for her by then? What might the future hold—if there really were a future? She lapsed into unconsciousness again and lay still and helpless under the white, crisp bedding.

Returning home was tinged with both hope and trepidation. Her mind raced along as she thought about just how she would manage without the support of the professional hospital staff with its emergency equipment. Comfort was found in the doctors' reassurance that she probably would be able to lead a productive life if she followed the carefully-planned regimen prescribed for her. Much depended upon the reduction of stress, medication, a strict diet and regular exercise.

In spite of the constraints, going home was a happy experience. When first she entered her apartment, she walked over to the living room window to the many plants and flowers. "They're alive" she said softly.

Calmly gazing out over the Potomac River, a view from her window, the sail boats were gliding across the surface. "How tranquilizing," she murmured. The sun reflected brightly off the water, almost blinding. "*It's great to be alive.* I missed this," said Bernice.

One afternoon in May Bernice found herself sitting in the office of her attorney. She needed to restructure her life in view of the catastrophic occurrences. Leaning forward on his desk, she earnestly asked, "And what of the future? I'm still breathing."

Attorney John Alexander ran his fingers through his mixed gray hair and leaned back in his leather upholstered chair. His blue eyes took on an intensity she had not seen before. "Bernice," he said kindly and quietly, "*do something while you're waiting to die.*"

"Do something while you're waiting to die." Bernice must not let her newly acquired frailty destroy her vivacious spirit. She might never again enjoy the level of energy she had reveled in over the years. Nonetheless that didn't mean she should remain a helpless invalid the rest of her days. Attorney Alexander knew that unless Bernice would rise to a challenge, she would wither at home until she was nothing but an insipid reminder of her former powerhouse self. She must not give up. She must find something to occupy her mind and challenge her spirit. She must allow herself no time to pine away in a rocking chair in a corner of her living room. Not Bernice. Her physical heart might stay crippled for the rest of her life, but her emotional heart must remain vigorous and well.

All the way home John Alexander's words echoed in Bernice's thoughts. "Do something while you're waiting to die." Which part of the sentence would she concentrate on? The "*waiting to die*" part or the "*do something*" challenge? The challenge lingered in her mind for days and weeks. "Do something while you're waiting to die." Sometimes she resented that advice. Sometimes she dismissed it. Sometimes the words seemed impossible as she lapsed into discouragement over her condition. But sometimes they energized her mind and piqued her imagination. "Bernice, do something while you're waiting to die." Would she heed her lawyer's advice? The choice was hers—and hers alone.

Attorney Alexander's advice set Bernice's feet on the road to Occoquan.

CHAPTER II

Occoquan: A Spectator's View

The initial visit to Occoquan Facilities I and II found Bernice unprepared for the conditions discovered there, and the repulsive feelings generated within. She was additionally distressed by the reality of a prison population noticeably youthful and overwhelmingly black.

Bernice found herself intimidated by the admission process, first confronted by those massive steel gates controlled, electronically, by an unseen operator. After entering one such gate she was required to await its closing, signaled by a loud "clanging," before passing through a second such gate. Momentarily, then, she was "trapped" between the two, and the experience for her was not comfortable. The searching of every inch of her pocketbook, as well as the "frisking" of her person constituted the ultimate invasion of her privacy and the pre-eminent attack upon her freedom. This is the reality of prison, she discovered; and it was not easily nor soon erased from her memory. Arrival at the chapel left Slaughter even less impressed and more distressed. The place was an eyesore.

The exterior appearance of the red-brick chapel was, at least, unappealing. It was indistinguishable from the neighboring buildings, ancient in its construction, unkempt and resembling a warehouse. As with all of the others, the windows of the chapel were protected by bars. The facade of the building was highlighted by a well-worn, dilapidated, peeling, once white wooden door, in desperate need of replacement.

The view of the chapel's interior caused Bernice to be offended and dumbfounded by its incredible condition. The brick walls were painted in an annoyingly pale shade of green. The ceiling was even less attractive. Hanging flourescent lights suspended from chains and pipe-like conduits, helped to create the warehouse appearance. An abundance of holes was the dominant characteristic of the composition board covering the ceiling. The floor was covered with block vinyl tile, with some squares visibly missing.

The chapel furniture, apparently donated, along with the remnants of a piano was seemingly victim of continuous hostile abuse, or at least careless use. It was a kind of desperate distress which overwhelmed Slaughter as her eyes encountered the horrid reality of this place.

For Bernice the decision to become a prison volunteer was the consequence of significant consideration. While thinking through the problem and wondering just how she would channel her limited energy in the future, Bernice considered volunteering to help with underprivileged children, but rejected that idea as she might become too attached to the little ones and go through separation anxiety.

In addition, she thought of working with the aged. This thought gave way to using her talent in a prison setting where it was also probable that her talent would be appreciated. Therefore, she consulted her family friend of long standing, Jaronza Ellis. Upon learning of

her interest in doing prison volunteer work, he then introduced Slaughter to the Occoquan Facility. The administration of the facility expressed its delight in
Slaughter's intended effort to gather together an inmates' choir. As for the inmates themselves, pleasure
and disbelief mingled in excited but wary expectation.
Their enthusiasm was high despite the repeated disappointment experienced while a succession of former
volunteers left without having achieved anything of
consequence, according to the residents. Notably elevated was inmate anticipation, in spite of their feeling
that a kind of potent opposition seemed to be thrown up
against previous religious volunteer attempts.

Any suspicions about the motivation or sincerity of
this new stranger were quickly dispelled. Reluctance
and hesitancy vanished as the inmates were attracted
by her piano playing. The men responded with enthusiastic singing; and, they expressed a readiness to participate, and an insistence that she return at the earliest
possible date.

The men welcomed their new friend, an accomplished pianist. She gave them an opportunity to get
away from their dormitories. She gave them a release, a
chance to lift their heads to the sky. She made them feel
like men instead of inmates.

Bernice knew and understood the magic of spiritual
music. Reared in her grandfather's church, Deanwood
First Baptist Church, far Northeast section of Washington, D.C., she learned early that music could be a kind
of sermon. As she played his favorite song, *"The Name
of Jesus Is So Sweet,"* she thought about George Washington Brent and the kind of man he was; he not only
preached the gospel, he lived it. Her grandfather was a
teacher, and Bernice was his star pupil.

Brent realized early in life, the importance of education. He believed that education was an absolute necessity for black folk. In pursuit of knowledge, he attended

Howard University in Washington, D.C., where he received bachelor and master degrees from the great black institution of higher education.

Brent used his wisdom to help and to motivate the black community. He realized that as a minister, he must strive to effectively meet the needs of his people.

One need he felt was to be a confidante of his granddaughter, Bernice, who would one day demonstrate her religion by helping those in need.

Bernice continued to play proudly as she reminisced about her grandfather who had been a spiritual and intellectual giant until his death. But, she realized that she was not at Deanwood First Baptist Church as a big bold cockroach waltzed across the piano.

It was at this time and place that Bernice's resolution to change the situation evolved. Upon seeing the dilapidated condition of the piano, now without pedals, she realized that the general conditions tended to depress her and probably had a similar effect upon the residents. She knew that she had to modify things in a hurry in order to carry out her mission—to form an inmates choir. She thought: *"The men eat in bricks and sleep in bricks so they should be able to worship in something other than unsightly brick."*

Now consumed by a personal perspective that does not allow for the witness of another's hurt without being moved by it, she resolved that her departure from the prison would leave the inmates there in an improved condition, superior to that which she discovered upon her arrival. Hers was now a mission; and she embarked upon it with all of the enthusiasm, conviction and energy of a determined missionary. *SOMETHING HAD TO BE DONE, SO SHE AND GOD, TOGETHER, WOULD DO IT.*

CHAPTER III

Music Heals the Fallen

With peaked excitement, light spirits and warmth, the prisoners stand abreast with curved fingers hooked through the chain-link fence that adjoins the chapel. They wave and call to the familiar volunteers, their fellow residents and to the invited guests who decorate the walkway. On this same walkway, the men are standing in parallel columns looking bright eyed and dignified in their light blue, white-trimmed choir robes and white bow ties. The men are meticulously groomed and seem to have a peaceful appearance. Some are humming to themselves as they prepare for their debut inside. Barbara A. Barnes, a volunteer, has been working with them hard and long for this performance.

Despite the light drizzle outside, the residents are ready to sing loud and strong at this Chapel Dedication Program. This is an occasion for residents to exhibit their finer qualities. It looks like Easter Sunday inside; the chapel is filled to capacity, with an over-flow outside. So the rest of the people look on to the garden around the chapel. They can see the multicolored flowers and green grass that cover what formerly was barren. The fragrance of the flowers seems enchanted by the huge floral heart formed with flowers and gravel with initials "BBS."

The men have dedicated this area to, Bernice B. Slaughter, from the residents of Occoquan Facilities I and II, May 29, 1985. Opposite the flower bed, the rising and falling water from the rented water fountain is symbolic of a refreshing, cleansing rain bringing forth needed change and renewed hope.

"*Behold, I make all things new.* I am Alpha and Omega—the beginning and the end. It is significant that the official first words spoken from the renovated chapel are the scripture of God's words," said Lutheran minister, Herbert A. Schwandt, to the crowded audience.

A resident comes up to a podium to welcome the visitors. "I didn't know that God could smile on me in jail," said John, the inmate. John's mother died when he was 13 years old. The theme of his message is a "rebirth," a rebirth in prison reform. "My mother has inspired me to do greater things than I have ever done," John said, as he referred to Bernice as his mother. "I thank God for sending Mrs. Slaughter to this institution. I thank the administration for allowing Mrs. Slaughter to come with things that never would be allowed otherwise—things that guys could jump up and kill each other with. We were able to use her husband's tools for this project. This is only the beginning of a great era in prison reform because Bernice Slaughter has connected spirituality with human life inside these prison walls. The next step will be establishing the same connection out in the community."

Next, Bernice's husband, Mr. James Slaughter comes to the podium. "I just want to say that since January of this year, a lot has taken place. Certainly, Bernice, my wife, had a dream. She has a unique way of getting people together to help in carrying out her dream. I have described her as a super ordinary lady with a unique mystique," James Slaughter said.

"As a person who has also been involved with this project, it has been quite rewarding to me. I have seen men behind prison walls reach out and find strength within themselves and use their skills to develop this project," said Mr. Slaughter, as he gestures toward various features within the chapel. What is needed here is continued community support. I have concluded that *people of goodwill with a noble goal acting with well planned, concerted activity, results in PROGRESS.* You can see progress here. Remember that *there is inherent beauty in a good idea because it spawns and nurtures other good ideas.* "Thank you," said Slaughter, as he left the podium feeling inspired.

The main speaker for this occasion is The Reverend Carey E. Pointer, Sr. "This is a significant hour in our history of the church. The times are pregnant with issues of vital importance. If we are to be successful in the task of rebuilding and in meeting the deepest needs of confused and suffering humanity, our methods must be reconstructed. We will learn to think creatively. The future usefulness of the concerned, the company of the committed, the community of faith, the guardian of the personal dimension against technological encroachment will depend upon her versatility to adapt herself to the circumstances which are so rapidly forming about her. The church is being judged by her deeds, not by her creeds. The question is: What are we really doing to uplift the fallen? Most of our church programs are pointing inward. How are we going to maintain the status quo? How are we going to take care of those who are out of the household of faith? Jesus said that we are to go into the world. I believe I heard Jesus say that I was in prison and you either visited or visited me not. What are we doing toward the advancement of mankind? What are we doing to save the lost? People are lost in so many ways. The majority of men don't care a lollipop about church doctrines. They are looking for practical translation of the spirit of Jesus Christ. We must prepare men to live, instead of preparing them to die. Our main objective is not to keep men out of hell, but to keep hell out of men," preached Pointer. The audience chorused with Amens.

"For if we keep hell out of men, we can keep men out of hell. Our aim is not to get men into heaven, but to get heaven into men. The institutions of religion, marriage, and business, are in a disarray. Things once held sacred have been desecrated. And while we are being exposed . . . . I have seen this beautiful chapel in the course of construction, before the work was really begun. I had no idea that Bernice wanted to renovate the entire chapel, buy an organ and do all the landscaping and painting and so on. (He smiles at Bernice sitting in the front of the chapel.) So, I joined with Bernice and other ministers in this greater task of rebuilding. In closing, my brothers and sisters, the real task is not renovating new buildings or building new facilities, as important as that may be, *the real job has to do with restructuring, rebuilding lives.* This building is a means to an end. And that is, to help the fallen, those who have lost hope and faith in the goodness of the universe. When life bears down on you hard enough, you can lose faith in the goodness of the universe. But as you continue the task of rebuilding lives, in the words of an old gaelic proverb, "May the road rise with you; may the wind always be at your back; and may God hold you in the hollow of his hand . . . May God bless you," remarked Pointer.

The audience was left with food for thought. Their faces seemed to look as if they were thinking, thinking about what the pastor had just said, and about how they, too, could help as Bernice and others had. *They knew that living would not be in vain, if they helped somebody.*

Then Bernice had her turn. "It's uplifting to reach the unreached," she said. "I thought I could be quiet today, but I cannot. Thank you for allowing me, Mr.

Palmer and Mr. Graves, to come down here and share my love with the residents.

I think God spared me for a reason; he brought me back to see this day. You have heard several times today that I came down here for the sole purpose of having just a little choir. But, when I saw the place, I did not like it. The place was laced with cigarette butts—unsightly, and when I played the piano, crumbling, dust-like particles would descend from the ceiling. And at one time, when I was playing, the chair in its weakened condition collapsed under me." The audience chuckles as Bernice tells her story.

"The place was not conducive for service. It did not lend itself to inspirational activity. I wanted the inmates to be effective and to be able to share with themselves and with their community their talents. Thanks to most of you for giving me your money because I could not always get your time. I appreciate all you have done to support this cause. I said to one of my doctors, and I see three of them out there in the audience, 'you know, yesterday I went down there and I declare it looked like they had dug my grave. Wasn't that mean?' She laughs and so does the audience in a very affectionate way. "I think the landscaping, by the way, is just fabulous. I think that the most beautiful thing I could think of in my life is a tribute of this nature. *Imagine, seeing your head stone and colorful flowers.* My mortician, my pastor, my choir and my organist are here. This is all that is needed to send me "home" feeling good." On that solemn note, Bernice concluded her speech.

The rest of the service was marked with praise for Bernice and what she had done for men who had gone unnoticed out in the world, but now have been touched by this petite berry brown lady.

Bernice understood that we are judged by how we treat the weakest of our society, not the strongest. We are judged by how we treat men in the pit of life. She

learned early in her grandfather's church what it was
to help somebody, especially in places like this place
where grown men cry. She wanted to touch the people
who are not always seen and seldom heard. She decided
to help those that had been lost; she wanted to help
those men who had been born in a dead end.

On the way back home, she recalled the airy spirituals that have engulfed the church. She remembered
playing at her grandfather's church at the age of 7
years old. Bernice could see Elsie Johnson's face, as
she would patiently teach her how to play the piano.
Then, she thought about when she was working her
way through school at Des Moines. But that wasn't
enough, so she went to Howard University to study music. Her two babies joyfully witnessed their divorced
mother's graduation.

So, it was really no wonder that Bernice used music
to help herself and others through the bad times. Mean-
while the "boys" were getting ready for their upcoming
performances.

The choir seems to take great pride in the fact that
they were performing for such a large audience. In addition, their voices had improved a great deal since Barbara Barnes had first started working with them. The
fact that they enjoyed singing also helped. For music,
seemed to be a sort of motivation for their life.

The choir sang a medley of spirituals. They led with
"Nobody Knows the Trouble I've Seen," and ended with
"Free at Last." It seems when the men sing, they are
free. They are no longer locked up behind the brick
walls, nor is their attention limited to their predicament. They seem to be emancipated by their singing.

It is no wonder that the choir has grown by talent
and numbers. Their pride is no longer in their pockets,
they have taken it and put it in their voices. Then sing
to God in the highest form of excellence that they can
achieve.

Chapel Dedication Program

A cross-section of the community joins with residents to celebrate the completion of the renovation project.

CHAPTER IV

Renovation

When Bernice walked into the 70 year old chapel building at the prison in early January 1985, she did so with the intention of organizing an inmates' choir. Looking around at the drab, dingy surroundings, she felt dismayed. An old piano sat in the corner, scratched and battered, loaded with cigarette butts. Some keys had been damaged and it was badly out of tune. There was no piano bench and when she attempted to sit on a chair in front of the piano, the chair collapsed and she fell to the floor.

How could she direct a choir in such a dismal atmosphere? *Remembering how her grandfather had built a church from the ground up with contributions and assistance from his congregation,* she decided that the chapel could be renovated using donations from area churches *and getting the prisoners to do the work.* She went home and began calling local ministers for donations toward the purchase of a new piano. Within three weeks, she had enough contributions to pay for the piano in full.

Along with a piano, there should be an organ. This would enhance the accompaniment for the choir, she thought. Again, she called church leaders and friends for funds. By mid-March, a beautiful Hammond organ was delivered.

When the renovation began in January, there was no pool of funds to purchase building materials, so the Slaughters used their own resources. Furring strips, plywood, molding, nails and paint were charged on their credit cards, loaded into their little '79 Chevette and taken out to the prison. Regulations required special permission to bring anything into the prison, and vehicles entering the gates were strictly inspected. The security staff carefully searched every inch of the vehicle for contraband. Once the vehicle passed inspection, it was driven to the chapel where the inmates quickly unloaded the materials. From the moment the first materials arrived, there was excitement among the men because they were being given something meaningful to do.

Work began on the interior walls. The drab green bricks were covered with plywood, then painted a soft, pale blue and trimmed with white. The pale blue was used throughout most of the interior because of its calming effect. As it turned out, this was also Bernice's favorite color.

Although Bernice knew nothing about renovating a building, "Charlie", an inmate did. He had worked as a carpenter and was familiar with electrical wiring. He was also familiar with the other inmates' skills. When someone was needed to work on pipes or install ceiling fixtures, he knew who to approach. Even those men who had no special skills clamored for a chance to assist with the renovation, so there was no shortage of labor. Each day, about 15 or 20 men could be found drilling, hammering, painting, sawing wood, and installing fixtures. The incessant boredom of being restricted to their dormitories made them welcome the

Photo by Bechet

The unimproved chapel exterior, with the exception of the wooden cross. The barren area shown is where the beautiful flower bed was created. This photo was taken on April 9, 1985.

change in routine and a chance for useful activity. Belief in the project, along with Bernice's charisma and personal concern for them, motivated the men to complete the entire renovation in five months, sometimes working 16 hours a day.

As the walls were being completed, work began on the ceiling. It was decided to install a drop ceiling and improve the building's lighting system. This required the installation of runners and framework as well as completely rewiring the ceiling. "Charlie" did most of the wiring for the ceiling assisted by "Sparky", another inmate who had experience as an electrician. Their

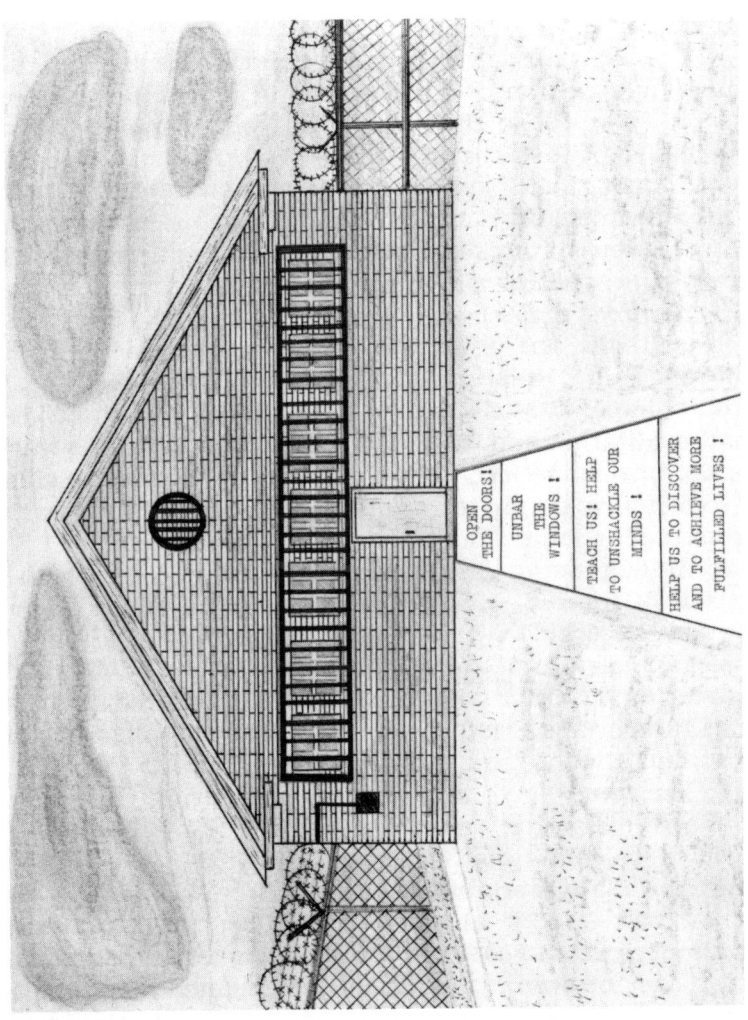

OPEN
THE DOORS!

UNBAR
THE
WINDOWS !

TEACH US! HELP
TO UNSHACKLE OUR
MINDS !

HELP US TO DISCOVER
AND TO ACHIEVE MORE
FULFILLED LIVES !

work was approved by departmental inspectors. Using 2' x 4' sheets of translucent, prismatic plastic, the men made the ceiling more even textured and the lighting much softer.

The floor became the next point of focus. A rich, dark blue carpet with tiny flecks of light blue was selected. Ironically, the salesman from whom Bernice purchased the carpeting was an ex-offender. When he learned what the carpeting was for, he was pleased and offered an additional discount on the price. By mid-April, enough funds had been solicited to purchase 220 yards of carpeting which the men installed.

Bernice never did anything halfway. She was pleased with the work being done, but her meticulous nature said it was not enough. She saw the need for a total chapel, a place that would be conducive to spiritual meditation and inspiration, as well as religious worship. The chapel needed a choir loft for the men to sing from and a pulpit for visiting ministers. This meant purchasing more wood.

Among many family members caught up in the spirit of the renovation project was Bernice's brother-in-law. He provided the men with a portable scaffold to use for installing the new ceiling. When he learned about the need for additional wood, he donated most of the lumber and 6000 nails. In February the men began building the loft and pulpit.

The men were closely supervised during the entire renovation period and the surveillance of their tools was very strict. Some tools were supplied by the prison, but the Slaughters brought many from home. Any of the tools—electrical saw, drills, framing squares, hammers—could easily be used as dangerous weapons.

Late one evening, an inmate telephoned the Slaughters at their residence and reported that "Sparky" had just been placed in "lockup." He explained that the problem was an apparently missing steel drill bit which could be converted into a lethal weapon. The drill bit

Photo by Bechet

The chapel in an advanced stage of completion. No longer do the steel bars grace the windows.

was last in the possession of "Sparky". The established fact was that "Sparky" was hurried out of the chapel by a correctional officer for the inmates count—roll call that occurs regularly during the day. Upon learning of the incident, the Slaughters rushed to the institution to intercede for "Sparky" whose attitude appeared to be too cooperative and helpful for this to be the case. They were greatly relieved to find that by the time they arrived at the prison, the correctional officers had found the drill bit where "Sparky" had left it. His release was direct and relief was instant. There remained, however, some hurt and disappointment in "Sparky" as the

whole episode seemed unfair to him. The trauma resolved itself with the demonstrated concern. The inmate's honesty typified the commitment of those
responsible for the renovation. *During the entire six-
month period, not one tool was misused or stolen.*

The spirit of cooperation and unity demonstrated
by the renovation crew impressed some of the prison's
correctional officers. They saw a difference in the
men's behavior. Every now and then an officer would
yell a few words of encouragement. Some did more.

One evening in May, as the men were installing two
exterior carriage lights, it grew dark and they did not
have enough light to continue drilling. An officer in a
nearby tower briefly focused his spotlight on the door
area, enabling them to finish installing the lights.

Renovation materials were sometimes donated by
retailers. A local paint store supplied 500 gallons of
paint for use throughout the prison. Other items for the
chapel were provided by individual supporters, very often the Slaughters' family and friends. Two family
members purchased a very elegant communion set for
the chapel. Bernice's physicians contributed gener-
ously towards purchasing the beautiful exterior door
made of cherry wood paneling with decorative block designs and a stained glass window. A mortician friend
purchased the interior door made of wood with glass
panels.

While many contributions for the renovation came
from churches, family, friends and supporters of the
project, others came from total strangers. Bernice was
home one evening when the phone rang.

"Mrs. Slaughter?"

"Yes."

"My name is "Margie Davis". My husband and I
heard you on a radio talk show and we want you to
know we really appreciate what you're doing for the
prisoners."

"Thank you, Mrs. Davis," Bernice responded. With
the continuous stress of raising funds and supervising

the renovation, it was encouraging to hear words of appreciation, especially from someone she had never met.

"Mrs. Slaughter, I was wondering if you could come over to my house and pick up a check?"

Bernice was unable to visit the lady until 4 days later. She was invited into the living room by a warm, elderly lady in her 70's. The lady's husband, also elderly, was confined to a wheel chair, but smiled at Bernice and extended his hand.

"John, this is Mrs. Slaughter," Mrs. Davis said. "You know Mrs. Slaughter, listening to you on the radio, I was expecting you to be bigger. But you're a tiny little thing."

Bernice smiled and offered her hand to John Davis. "Mr. Davis, it's kind of you and your wife to call and give your support."

"We admire what you are doing and we've been praying for you—that God will bless your efforts," he said. They apologized for their meager surroundings, explaining that they did not have much money.

"Mrs. Slaughter, here's our check. It's not a lot, but we hope it will help."

Bernice took the check for $5.00. Looking around the sparsely furnished room and Mr. Davis in the wheel chair, she realized with how much sacrifice the check had probably been written. She fought back the tears.

"Mrs. Davis, you can be sure the guys in prison will appreciate this as much as I do. I'm looking forward to telling them about your interest in them," she said.

The Davises beamed with satisfaction. Before leaving, Bernice walked over and hugged them both.

And then, the next evening a call came from a friend, Tina. "Bernice," she said, "My husband just passed. He's been quite ill. I appreciate so much the care and concern you are showing the inmates. I am asking that in lieu of flowers, contributions be sent to you to help in that project." The total contribution of $1200.00 was applied to the cost of the pews. Upon notification of this deed, the inmates immediately sent ex-

An exterior view of the completed chapel. The newly prepared flower
bed is in the lower left-hand corner.

pressions of sympathy. One inmate sent her a beautiful
handbag which he made from cigarette packs.

Overcoming challenges has been a way of life for
Bernice Slaughter since she was a little girl. When she
was seven years old and learning to play the piano,
Grandpa Brent told her that in a few weeks she was to
play a hymn, "The name of Jesus is so Sweet," at
church. He had high expectations of his granddaughter
and made it clear that if she had to "play without fingers", she would play. She nervously waited for the day
to arrive and when it did, she played with ease and con-
fidence. Her grandfather was pleased and rewarded her
with a $100.00 war bond.

"I did what I was told the way I was told to do it,"
she said, recalling the day her parents bought her a

typewriter and told her she would learn how to type. Bernice was only nine, but they said that she may one day have to earn a living by typing. So she became a proficient young typist. Whenever a challenge was presented to her and her brother, they were given no choice about whether they would succeed. It was expected of them. "My parents were very particular. They did not like to be embarrassed by their children. They insisted that all the things they required would be useful later in life," she said.

Another characteristic that Ella and Earl Brent instilled in their children was the importance of helping people in need. Her grandfather and father spent a lot of time visiting those less fortunate. "I've always tried to pick others up," she stated. "To find a situation where someone was worse off than I was and help them. This is very rewarding though many times painful."

Changes brought by the renovation project were not confined to the chapel building. There was a noticeable difference in the behavior of the inmates who worked on the project. Tensions eased and conflicts among the men were greatly reduced. On one occasion, when the Slaughters drove up with a carload of building materials, an inmate, "Billy" handed over a letter which he wanted to read at the upcoming dedication ceremony. In the letter he explained how his attitude and life had changed since working with the renovation crew. He wanted to publicly express his gratitude for being involved in such an uplifting experience. "This chapel is not the only thing that's being renovated," he said.

"Charlie Draper" was perhaps the hardest and most faithful worker on the renovation crew. He wept when the volunteers gave him a little recognition on his birthday. When the chapel was completed, he received another surprise. He had two missing front teeth (the result of an altercation somewhere) and was very self-conscious about smiling. A dental technician who had supported the project financially heard about "Draper"

and made him a special gift of a partial plate with two
new teeth at no cost. Other inmates also developed very
special relationships with Bernice during the course of
the renovation.

Highlighting the chapel ceiling is a mural depicting
God's love extended to all mankind. It was painted by
an inmate, who visibly through his works was extremely talented and humble. Bernice saw him walking
the grounds one day carrying a huge drawing pad. She
asked him about it and he explained that he loved to
draw. He was then invited into the chapel where he
showed her a sample of his artistic ability. A week later,
he began work on the mural. An image was projected
into the plexiglass and painted prior to placing it in the
ceiling. It took several weeks for him to complete the
work.

"Pat Hawkins", a 45 year old inmate loved to sing.
His tenor voice was beautiful and melodious. He loved
alcohol. Alcohol had no place for him. As a result, he
was incarcerated. When he was released, Bernice took
him to a church. Upon introduction and a statement
seeking support of the ex-offender, he was graciously
received by the congregation. Hawkins told the church
of his desire to keep the image of Christ blinking before
him. He then sang a song "Precious Lord, Take My
Hand." Tears began to flow from many eyes.

A member of the Slaughter family assisted him in
finding a place to live, and a job (shampooing dogs). The
church gave him money for transportation to and from
the job.

Loving to sing, Hawkins would frequently serenade
the dogs as he brushed them. People passing the dog
grooming parlor would often hear *a singing man and
barking dogs.*

His expressed hope was giving up alcohol and turning his life around. The police found him lying in the
street drunk one day. He was returned to prison. He remains spiritually active.

Photo by Bechet

This flower bed is dedicated to Bernice. The inscription on the masonry tablet reads: "A tribute to Bernice B. Slaughter, As an Expression of Love, From the Residents of Occoquan Facilities I and II, May 29, 1985."

Recognizing the difficulties of transition from prison into the community, Bernice was disappointed about Hawkins, however, her faith did not diminish. "He'll be okay," Bernice declared.

"Ray Brooks" attended chapel services regularly. He enjoyed the peaceful, spiritual atmosphere away from the conflicts of prison. His attendance and participation in the spiritual enrichment programs was unsurpassed. Bible study seemed to be his chief priority. Asked if he would accept the job as the chapel custodian, he anxiously accepted. The community paid him monthly. With pride, he cleaned the chapel each day. He

policed the area—demanding that everyone would respect the building and its contents.

Unlike many men in Occoquan who were there for
various crimes, "Brooks" was imprisoned as a result of
alleged negative behavior arising out of excessive alcohol intake. He says that heavy intake of alcohol was due
to insurmountable domestic problems. His quiet, pleas-
ant manner greatly impressed many. EVOL (Every Volunteer of Love) Prison Ministry collected funds for
further legal defense. He is grateful. At this time he has
been released—doing well.

—————————— C H A P T E R V ——————————

Special Programs

For too many years, there has been a wide gulf between the prison community and the larger society of which the inmates are an integral part. *Could it be that they have been put into a corner . . . and too often forgotten?* Special programs such as those described provide opportunities for community folk to "rub shoulders" with prisoners in a wholesome way. *When it is demonstrated that some prison residents are talented and intelligent, trained and trainable, the public may have reason to view them differently.* This may well be an added consequence of the special program activities.

The Pre-Dedication Program

The Pre-Dedication Program of May 17, 1985, recognized individuals and their accomplishments. It also provided an opportunity for many residents to attend who might not be present for the Dedication scheduled for May 29, 1985.

The prelude selection, "It is Well With My Soul," had particular meaning for those who shared in the program.

"God has Smiled on Me," said the resident as he started his welcome address. In those words, he was echoing the words the choir had just sung. He continued, "The sun is shining bright even though it is cloudy outside." Thanking the audience for having come, he pointed out that he had lost his mother 23 years earlier and Mrs. Slaughter had become like a mother to him. He then mentioned that the honorees, Revs. Thomas and Angela Turner were inspirational people. "They have done so much for us", said the inmate.

The Turners spoke about how impressed they were with what was being done and that they wanted to be contributors. They also appreciated that such a great concession was made for them today. "We are leaving for the 'Holy Land' in just a few more days. We cannot be here for the regular dedication." They recognized the hard work done by the residents in completing the renovation project. They ended their talks by reminding the inmates that they looked forward to working more with them in the future. This brought cheers from the residents.

"The Golden Hour" is here. Today is Friday, October 11, 1985, the day set aside for the dedication of the chapel pews. This is the culminating conclusion of the monumental task of soliciting an additional eight thousand dollars. Once again it is time for Thanksgiving. The newest addition to the chapel is the brand new white pews trimmed with walnut. The blue upholstered seats and backs do blend well with, and are complementary to the chapel interior decor.

The crowded sanctuary has been stirred up by the opening prayer, offered by Herbert A. Schwandt. The place is left buzzing; folk everywhere are responding verbally, emotionally to an electrifying prayer. And, the chapel choir only accelerated the excitement with its

Photo by Bechet

An inmate who cultivated a garden hands Bernice a tomato that he produced. The garden idea was inspired by the chapel renovation and the landscaping in the chapel area.

rendition of "The Lord's Prayer" before this standing room only audience.

New York City's James Henry is enthusiastic and animated in his exquisitely skilled performance of a piano solo, "The Dedication" by Schuman-Liszt. So movingly does he accomplish his rendition that Slaughter is caused to reminisce about the struggles shared by the two of them as students at Howard University's College

Photo by Brooks

There is standing room only as residents attend the Pew Dedication
Ceremony. Said one inmate, "I didn't know that God could look on me
in jail".

of Fine Arts. Separated since those days, these two
have been reunited after twenty years by a national network news report of Slaughter's work.

Inmate "Ray Brooks" is visibly overwhelmed by the
intensity of emotion on this occasion; and his attempt
at reading the scripture lesson is momentarily, yet un-
derstandably, interrupted while he regains composure.
The crowd is notably impressed with his effort and ap-
plauds its approval. Returning to his seat, he is followed by the main speaker for the day.

"All the King's Horses And All The King's Men" is
the title of the sermon offered by David James Jackson.
This ingeniously prepared message has an unmistak-
able impact on the audience. Jackson weaves a story of

the biblical dry bones into a parallel situation at this Occoquan prison facility.

". . . The Lord asked it of him: 'Ezekiel, can these bones live?" Jackson announces. "The answer is resident in the consequence of Slaughter's effort, well recognized across the world. Indeed, there is the possibility of rejuvenating the lives of warehoused inmates, and today's spectacle is proof of it".

Throughout the sermon, Pastor Jackson, addresses Bernice and the inmates as though God were speaking directly to them, instead of to Ezekiel, giving them assurance that "In Him there is no failure." The repetition of the statement increased its power. Pastor Jackson, well familiar with the many obstacles, the apparent subtle sabotage, the intangible resistance and anxiety generated by the project, further assured them: "After a while, Bernice, your sorrow will turn into joy. Remember in Him there is no failure." With raised voice, approaching a crescendo and clenched hands clearly revealing the intensity of his feeling, and beads of perspiration stealing down his face, he further declares: "Never mind, Bernice, that conditions are less than optimal; never mind that resistance is plentiful; in Him there is no failure! . . . If you will hear what He says; and if you will do what He tells you to do, "ALL THE KINGS HORSES AND ALL THE KINGS MEN CANNOT STOP YOU."

Partly through the recurring question "Can these bones live?", Pastor Jackson makes the sermon *live*. It is a veritable masterpiece which leaves the audience enthralled, pensive, inspired and convinced that these bones *can* live." Indeed, these bones *should* live. These bones *must* live. What other hope is there in a place *where grown men cry?*

Moments pass while the residents and guests regain their composure as the chapel choir prepares itself to sing. By the same token, the chapel choir is so motivated as it sings the next selection:

"Over on the Other Shore"

Friends all left me a long time ago,
I had not a one to be seen,
Because I had decided deep within my soul,
That I would live another way.

Satan keeps rocking me from side to side.
Like a ship on an angry sea.
And I keep watching and waiting for that happy day.
When the Lord will deliver me.

Chorus: Going away on a journey and
I won't be back no more
He promised me a starry crown.
Over on the other shore.

Going to meet in the middle of the air.
Going to jump and shout for joy,
Put on my robe, walk the streets of gold,
over on the other shore.
Going to meet with Jesus, sorrows will be no more,
Always be contented, over on the other shore.

Their syncopated gospel tune, "Over On The Other
Shore," maintained the spirit of hope.

With the organ now humming its soft strains, the
audience now hears: "My Lord, my Lord, how excellent
is thy name. We are living witnesses, walking testimony, that through divine aid and human effort,
through holy blood and human sweat, this chapel has
moved from the lofty imagination and mind of Bernice
Slaughter, to the level grounds of reality." Pastor
Eugene Weathers is now in the midst of the prayer of
dedication for the pews. "We dedicate these pews to
thee," he continues. "Let your glory fill this place and

sanctify these pews for your service." Once again the crowd is emotionally charged, brought to its feet in joyous exuberance. "We pray that this house will be a 'stop-by' station for the least, the last and the lost. We pray that this house will be a service station for the depressed, deranged, despondent and the down and out. We pray that this house will be a sailing marina for the young men who have had collisions with the law . . . and folk whose souls need to stand. I know the glory must go to God. God uses all of us as his instruments; and he has used Bernice Slaughter as his instrument. Join me now in giving her a standing ovation." There was a memorable response. Bernice now approaches the podium.

"Ladies and gentlemen and my guys," Slaughter speaks after a standing ovation. "I am so happy today . . . that I am overwhelmed. I have talked so much since January, I am about out of words by now." David Decatur, Administrator, is then given a plaque by her, as the religious volunteer coordinator, for his cooperation in the project. Arthur Graves (former administrator) receives a plaque in recognition of his crucial role in the early phases of the project. Barbara Barnes is another toward whom gratitude is directed. Slaughter acknowledges that Barnes' work with the choir freed her to devote full attention to the chapel project.

Having concluded her brief remarks with difficulty, seemingly overwhelmed by the magnitude of the day, yet struggling to conceal the gradually flowing tears of joy, Slaughter is sent to her seat with the deafening applause of a standing ovation.

Eyes all over the place are still tearful as the chapel choir prepares for its closing selection: "Give Us This Day." Ordinarily Barbara Barnes is the sole accompanist for the choir. However, on this occasion, she is joined by Slaughter, at the piano. A powerful aura was witnessed around the room. The blending of voices and

Photo by Brooks

A mirthful moment during the Pew Dedication Ceremony. It was necessary to place additional chairs in the aisles.

instruments, along with the particular message embodied in the song, made for a memorable occasion.

> *"Give us this day, our daily bread,*
> *you said you would supply all our needs*
> *according to your riches.*
> *I have but to ask*
> *and I shall receive.*
>
> *To go on from here,*
> *and share this love you gave to me*
> *to show someone who's lost,*
> *and help them find their way,*
> *their way to truth and faith*
> *so they can be free, like me, free like me.*

> *Lord, we need your love,*
> *Lord, we need your peace,*
> *Lord, we need your joy, this day."*

Although the choir sang well, the lyrics seemed to add a plaintive mood, undeniably emanating from the depths of their souls. These singers are now demonstrating to a diversified audience their discovery of freedom in the midst of confinement. And for the discovery, they thank God for Bernice.

Many feelings and comments are evoked by the combined performance. "I couldn't help myself," the Bahamian, Harcourt Bastian, reported. Looking around, one could see a number of people gently dabbing at their eyes . . . without restraint and embarrassment. Perhaps they, too, discovered that *this is where grown men cry.*

The Christmas Concert

Hundreds of hands explode in thunderous applause to register their approval. The vocalist while performing his program of songs, projects the depth of his sincerity to an eager audience. The extended fingers of his, becoming clenched fists attached to gesturing arms; squinting eyes and a contorted face are additional evidences of a momentous occasion at this Occoquan Facility. He sings of the Christ, and of the two thieves suspended from their undignified crosses. One thief entreats: "Remember me, remember me; I want to be forgiven for the sins I have committed. *Lord, please . . . please . . . please, remember me!"* The audience is listening to every word and following every movement as this musical rendition does gradually conclude. Once more, enthusiastically applauding hands say: "Well done!"

The resounding approbation is mainly the response of hundreds of inmates present in the audience. All have assembled here because this gymnasium is the

only place in the Occoquan Facilities I and II where
more than five hundred men can be accommodated.
Notwithstanding that the bone-chilling weather outside
has lowered the temperature inside, renowned record-
ing artist *Wintley Phipps* has generated an enthusias-
tic response from this audience. Instead of being in
California where he has important commitments, this
December 21, 1985, he is performing in a special
Christmas concert for prison inmates. This is the
Wintley Phipps who sang at the Democratic National
Convention. This is the Wintley Phipps who believes in
prison reform; and this performance is the proof.

Facing the stage, there is an impressive view of the
Christmas-tree-decorated stage and the huge "WEL-
COME WINTLEY PHIPPS" sign suspended from the
ceiling. The concert starts with volunteer Slaughter
calling for complete attention of the audience. Next,
Pastor David James Jackson, in a deeply resonant
voice and deliberate manner, offers the invocation: "For
the privilege of this gathering, Almighty God, we do
now pause to speak something of our thanksgiving . . .
for the time and quality of service rendered to these
ones by Wintley Phipps . . . Amen."

The introduction of Wintley is done by James
Slaughter: "Ladies and gentlemen, good evening . . . It
is my distinct honor and pleasure to present to you, Mr.
Wintley Phipps." The appearance of Phipps on stage is
heartily received as this is his *second* appearance at
Occoquan in two months. In his sonorous baritone-bass
voice, the artist, with an orchestral accompaniment begins: "What a glorious day . . . I just want to praise the
Lord." By the time the song ends the audience is fully
involved and totally responsive.

The 165-pound, medium sized vocalist presents
more of his repertoire when he sings "I Choose You
Again and Again," slowly with feeling and with meaning, "Good evening everyone, Can you hear me? I want
to say, first of all, thank you for the privilege of being

here. The music we're doing here is not like other music in that it doesn't mean a thing unless you *hear* the message in it (touching his ear for emphasis). The most important thing that we are going to try to do tonight is to get a message across. *You see, music is the most powerful means of impressing the mind.* And, that's why I want to share with you tonight, music which God has given me through the years. The song that I just sang . . . is my testimony. The message is: *Lord, if I had my life to live over again, I would choose you again and again and again.* Because you mean so much to me, I choose you again and again."

The next song to be introduced is syncopated and contemporary. "This is a song I sang on *Saturday Night Live,*" Phipps commented. It is a song that says if you do anything wrong, there is an almost immediate sense of emptiness as though God has turned his back on you and is subject to walk away. The only way to get around it and to be at peace is to come clean and say, "God, you give me one more chance and say you love me. We all know that we need to know that we are loved by one another and that we are loved, most of all, by God. God, tell me again that you love me." Singing begins again.

". . . Lord you know I need to feel you by my side . . . the love you hold for me will never die" (He holds the word "die" so long, it seems it will never die). Mr. Phipps is rewarded with another impressive ovation. Now referring to the song that he sang at the Democratic National Convention, the performer sings again.

The song is Ordinary People, Phipps addresses the audience: "I am so glad God uses ordinary people, he uses people just like you and me, who are willing to do as he commands, God uses people who will give him all, it doesn't matter how small you all may be . . . little becomes much when you place it in the Master's hand."

At the conclusion of his song he asks: "How many of you heard Jesse Jackson's speech at the Democratic National Convention last year? God gave me the privilege to sing that song right after his speech. The message was 'you don't have to compromise to be recognized'; just be faithful to God. He is your best agent. If you stay right here in prison and if you're faithful to God, you will watch him open doors, you will watch him do things for you that are just out of this world."

After completing a Caribbean Christmas song, Phipps went on to say: "You know, I preached this morning. I was talking to some people and I said 'some people think that Christmas is about toys and trinkets. They pay more attention to the birthday than the one who was born on Christmas.' The most amazing thing about Christmas is a word called condescension. It means to come from way up high and to go way down low. That is what Jesus did. He was a king in heaven. He came way down for us."

Pastor Phipps, turning his attention now from the songs said: "To those who decorated the place and put up the signs, *'fantastic'! thank you!"* (The audience emphatically voiced its approval.) "And to the administrator, thanks for the privilege of sharing here. And of course, Mrs. Slaughter, please give her a big hand for if it were not for her, I wouldn't have been able to come here." (Loud applause.) This is not the end, however, for there is more in store for the audience.

Phipps introduces his next song by explaining that: "There was a man who felt like he wanted to be saved and this was the last day of his life. As he was dying, he prayed a prayer. I want to share that song with you:

> *"A thief lay dying on a cross, and he knew all along, that he had done wrong, now for his debts, he must die.*
> *But as he saw the Christ, with his blood flowing down, he knew he had found, the one who could save his soul.*

> *So he cried 'remember me when you come into*
> *   your kingdom, oh Lord, remember me.*
> *When you talk to your father, and tell him that I*
> *   know, I've not been as he wants me to be . . .*
> *Lord, please remember me'."*

Moving from the song to a preaching mode, Phipps says: "Remember that man has his kingdom and God has his kingdom. Don't miss out on God's kingdom. The only thing that matters is the kingdom of God. That is why the thief said Lord, remember me. For his closing he sings:

> "Shower me with your love, Oh Lord,
>   shower me with your love,
>   shower me with your holy love,
>   shower me with your h-o-l-y love."

(Inviting the audience to participate, he continues as the inmates sing along with him.) The gymnasium is filled, vibrating with one massive voice, joyously singing lyrics directed toward God himself.

And so the evening's occasion is concluded as hundreds of standing men gather together, each one grasping the hand of another as the benediction is being pronounced by Pastor Herbert Schwandt. Many of the inmates then depart the gym reluctantly. A selected few remain behind to secure the equipment. There are frequent expressions of gratitude for the performance and numerous requests for autographs, to which Phipps graciously complies. This is the biggest event yet sponsored by the volunteers associated with the chapel renovation program.

Summary

The foregoing material has detailed most of the salient points about the series of Special Programs that were presented in the chapel. Each program had as its focus the observance of a particular phase of the project or a particular event during the year. A great amount of effort was put forth to achieve the completion of the various phases of the project.

The Pre-Dedication Program (May 17, 1985) recognized individuals and their accomplishments. It also provided an opportunity for many residents to attend who might not be accommodated at the Dedication scheduled May 29, 1985.

The Chapel Dedication Program on May 29, 1985, was a larger celebration of the completion of the renovation which was accomplished within five months. It, too, was an occasion for giving thanks to the Creator for the important changes that had been effected. It was enhanced by media coverage which, hopefully, would win support for the movement designed to bring a richer, more wholesome experience to the incarcerees.

The Pew Dedication Program (October 11, 1985) constituted another milestone in that the total renovation had been brought to fruition. The acquisition of the pews and the pulpit furniture represented the culmination of an extensive effort to obtain funds to purchase these items. This also provided an opportunity to have talented individuals from *outside* the institution to show their interest and to give their support. Through Pastor Jackson's stirring sermon, one could see the parallel situations as God used Ezekiel and Bernice as instruments to initiate action.

The Wintley Phipps Christmas Concert also was an attempt to encourage the inmates and to brighten their hopes for the future. The timing of the program was important, too, as it was presented during a season when many people tend to go into depression. Mr. Phipps had postponed important trips out of town in order to render the special entertainment.

Whereas in the very beginning the number of residents attending the chapel *prior* to the renovation project usually numbered fewer than five individuals, the numbers increased manifold when the organized programs started. When community ministers and their choirs began coming, "standing room only" audiences became a common occurrence. There were opportunities for more residents to visit the chapel for spiritual experience. There also were opportunities for members of the community and government officials to learn more about what was done at Occoquan Facilities I and II Chapel and the affect it had on inmates, i.e., a calming, meditative effect, thus reducing ever-present tension among inmates. It is hoped that the favorable publicity helped to point up *the urgent need for prison reform.*

CHAPTER VI

Spiritual Enrichment Program

"Interpreting the Divine Word Through Profound Service"

A Spiritual Enrichment Program at Occoquan helps to elevate the morale and quality of life for imprisoned human beings. *It offers genuine caring, manifested through practical assistance.* Its volunteers conduct chapel programs, pray with prisoners, work with them individually and in groups, and perform various services to help solve personal problems.

The program, begun in July 1985, now involves more than fifty-one churches and their congregations. During the Chapel Renovation Program, prisoners had told volunteers that they are frustrated and anxious because they cannot manage important personal affairs. Not only do they often need someone on the outside to act for them, but they also need technical know-how, encouragement, and contact with people in the community.

From the beginning, the Chapel Program sponsors had planned to invite ministers from the Washington,

D.C., metropolitan area to conduct services. Church members and choirs were also encouraged to participate, and the program quickly evolved. Some groups donated Bibles, hymnals or literature. A number of persons volunteered to conduct classes in Bible study. Regular Sunday services were soon joined by services on Wednesdays and Saturdays.

When church members went to Occoquan for services, they met the inmates. The psychological gulf between the "inside" and "outside" began to shrink. Communication was two-way, with prisoners and church members learning from each other.

In becoming better acquainted with the imprisoned men, church congregations become more aware of the anxieties, uncertainties and personal problems incarcerees face. Volunteers get their first sense of the frustrations and restraints when they must sign up long before the actual date of a service at Occoquan. Upon arrival at the Check Point inside the institution, they wait to see that their names match those on the approved visitor list. They register and submit to a "frisking" to make sure they carry no contraband. They are led to the chapel by a correctional officer. After they are seated, the Control Center notifies the dormitories to send interested residents to the chapel.

Thus, by the time services begin, church members know a little of what it is like to be behind bars. They may already begin to feel cut off from the outside world or frustrated from the cumbersome procedures of prison life.

Since the absence of stabilizing community ties could be a major cause of recidivism, the Spiritual Enrichment Program developed a Sponsorship Program in which individual churches adopt one or more inmates well in advance of the man's release date. *The purpose of the program is to establish a link between the incarceree and the community.* While a man is still in prison, the minister is expected to see that contact is maintained between the congregation and its adoptee. Hopefully, he will encourage them to support the man through crisis counseling, a small allowance while in prison, employment assistance, help to obtain necessary clothing, food and a place to live.

Frequently ministers and their congregations are initially fearful of entering a penal institution. For example, several ministers have made such comments as, "Mrs. Slaughter, I'll have to get my 'nerves' together before I can go in there and preach. I'd better say a prayer first."

A minister might sit in the office and meditate before delivering his sermon. While sitting quietly in the room adjacent to the chapel sanctuary, he can hear testimonies and hymns presented by residents. The hymns and gospel songs they sing would be well known to his own congregation.

Ministers and their congregates soon discover that they have much in common with the prisoners. Contrary to some people's worst fears, the prisoners at the chapel are not concentrating on "ripping off" anybody. Their interests transcend violence. They want fellowship. They want to hear the Divine word and to praise God.

When the very personal and heartfelt outpourings of residents combine with those of members of the outside community, *a vital human and common bond forms.* Mutual acceptance grows as the services progress. This is most noticeable after residents approach the altar for prayer and to dedicate their lives to Christ. A number express deeper yearnings for spiritual development by requesting baptism.

The smooth functioning of the program depends upon adequate planning and coordination. Extensive preparation of ministers, choirs and congregation is made prior to their arrival.

When a minister accepts the invitation to conduct a chapel service, Bernice Slaughter, the Volunteer Coordinator, or an Assistant Coordinator, mails an Institutional Access List to the Church. The pastor must list the name and address of each person who is to accompany him on this form and promptly mail it back to the Coordinator. The prison Administrator's office then checks the list for approval of those visiting Occoquan.

At least one community volunteer is present at the chapel to receive guests and to introduce the minister and his choir, if any. Residents are told pertinent facts about the minister, the church, and the kind of support the church has given and will give.

The presence of volunteers in this initial visit is crucial as they are familiar with rules and procedures governing the conduct of services and because they can help break the ice between the residents and the visiting church members. *Volunteers help to coordinate the orderly movement of residents and guests.* (Guests remain seated while residents depart the chapel at the end of the service so the men can return to the dormitories promptly.)

Dormitory representatives are an important link between the chapel volunteer staff and the residents. An alarming number of "glitches" once occurred when men were supposed to appear in the chapel for scheduled functions. Now dormitory representatives can be trusted to post important notices in the dormitories regarding planned programs. They also can be counted on to furnish feedback on selected speakers and services and valuable constructive criticism.

The Spiritual Enrichment Program is now viewed as one of the most important structural supports of the bridge linking the prison and the community. Possibly, it is a model for prison reform.

David Decatur, Administrator of Occoquan Facilities I and II declared: "There has been nothing to parallel the success of this program."

The Spiritual Enrichment Program has provided large numbers of men the opportunity to obtain emotional release through participation in services. They have also learned that members of the larger community are more acutely aware of their plight and that individuals and groups were willing to respond to their need. The sponsorship arrangement gives them additional hope that they can make adequate adjustments after release.

The Spiritual Enrichment Program is comprehensive and solidly based in the love and spiritual vision of its participants. Often, it provides a man his only positive aspect to incarceration.

Building a fulfilling life after prison is always difficult. Genuine caring on the part of volunteers helps the men to realistically assess their problems, discover appropriate solutions, and commit themselves to necessary changes. These loving bonds affirm each man's feelings of worth and value. They can change his perceptions of hopelessness or futility into a vision that will lead him into a fulfilling and spiritual life.

CHAPTER VII

"Impact"

The Occoquan Spiritual Enrichment Program is a dramatic example of the powerful and positive impact the effort of a few may have upon many. It began simply with one resourceful and versatile individual who wanted to put the word of God into action by sharing her musical gifts.

An increasingly close association with Occoquan inmates did reveal to Slaughter a reality that the prison walls were isolating and restricting a great deal of talent, which if meaningfully utilized, might significantly heighten the self-image of the individual inmate. Much of the labor involved in the renovation project came from the inmates themselves. Together she and they worked—sometimes day and night. Those many working hours spent together did foster a kind of intimate relationship between them. Consequently, the two—Slaughter and the inmates—became an indispensable part of each other's lives. For the inmates, Slaughter became their "Mom"; and to Slaughter, the inmates became her "boys."

Having been deeply touched by the men of Occoquan and their families, hers became a clear view of the magnitude of the situation and the scope of the necessary solutions which would demand the involvement of many others.

Since May 1985, many congregations have worshipped with the inmates in the Occoquan chapel, convincingly demonstrating to the prison population the concern for them by the outside community.

During the actual chapel reconstruction process, the role of the volunteers became significant. Not only did they give support, they furnished bibles, cards and stationery. In addition, it was necessary for volunteers to be on duty much of the time as the departmental regulations required that responsible persons be on duty while inmates worked at their tasks.

Whatever a volunteer's contribution may be, his or her concern and effective participation may often be sufficient motivation for an inmate to cause a reassessment of his circumstance as well as his future prospects; particularly since many, themselves, have been victims of criminal activity. Members of the community are numbered among those ones willing to serve. Prior to becoming a religious volunteer, Bernice, too, was victimized. However, this was not a deterrent to volunteer service. Even though the vast majority of service was geared to men who still were within the confines of the prison compound, some attention still was given to men who recently were released from the institution. Many of them needed continuing service.

"Those who bring sunshine into the lives of others cannot keep it from themselves," said Sir James Barrie. That quotation appears to have considerable validity for volunteers, as they are affected by their own interaction with inmates. It seems they are more able to experience more in-depth relationships with residents, and are able to see just a bit more of the social, economic, spiritual, psychological and political implications involved. Some indications of how much they have gained by giving to the program include such comments and experiences as:

"It gives me reason for being."

"It is good to know that you have talent that is beneficial to others."

"Working with the men helps me to realize a greater range of possibilities within myself."

"I am pleased to know that I am doing God's will to help His children."

"Much of the joy of living comes from helping others."

"It is important to help people to recognize their responsibilities in creating the predicaments they now are in."

"Being associated with such a worthy cause gives me a new sense of pride."

"No matter how insignificant we may feel, there is always something we can do to help someone who is in trouble."

"Trouble is no respecter of persons; it comes to everyone at some time."

"I cannot scorn them; it could have been me."

"We are learning a new application of the statement that in unity there is strength."

"There is a lot of insight that we can get from residents."

"Their problems often are just like ours."

"God does not discriminate against the physically inconvenienced."

"Positive belief in myself can help on the road to success."

"To stop moving is to start dying. I consider my physical inconvenience an unequivocable challenge."

"Here's devotion to promoting understanding between the community and the incarceree, through the help of God."

To start any new program in a penal institution requires official support, which often is not provided. It was important to impress prison officials with the possibility that the proposed program would be beneficial enough to offset administrative difficulties. Security was a primary concern as the program would involve many volunteers coming into the prison and a large number of prisoners moving into and out of the chapel.

Some correctional staff welcomed the volunteers and cooperated freely with them. Programs like this, they thought, were appropriate and long overdue. Because the tension of chapel-going inmates appeared to be greatly reduced, some staff discovered their jobs to be a bit less difficult. *One staff member pointed out that at times, they too, had problems with relationships that paralleled those of inmates and that they, too, needed spiritual rejuvenation.*

Other staff members have an opposing view. Some believe help for inmates to be a low priority; some believe that a man is in prison to be harshly punished and that their job is to inflict harsh punishment. As a result, some do not see the worth of spiritual programs. A number of inmates allege that a few correctional officers, even on the supervisory level, scheduled highly explicit sex films to compete with the Spiritual Enrichment Program in the chapel and that they found this to be offensive.

Feedback from various sources revealed that officials were unprepared for the results of the program. *Widespread cynicism and behind-doors-chuckling changed to astonishment,* however, as resources and resolves moved the chapel project along at a rapid and consistent pace. As Mr. Arthur Graves, former Administrator of Occoquan Facilities I and II, pointed out, "She made a believer out of me."

Hundreds of inmates have participated in the chapel program at Occoquan. Some of them have sought sponsorship by a pastor and/or a congregation. Some are still in prison awaiting release, and some have successfully (so far) made a transition to life outside. Few have returned to prison after release.

One measure of the program's impact is the testimonials of a few inmates. One says, "As a result of this involvement, I have learned something which remains constantly on my mind . . . there are people who care and if one just takes the initiative to care about him or herself, positive results are bound to manifest." Efforts to bring about for inmates a positive transition into society have been pronounced.

Other testimonies of inmates seem to suggest that hope, through religion, is heightened:

"The program provides loving care that helps develop awareness of who you are and what you really need to do to survive."

"What she gave me in the program helped give me something to hold on to. It helped me to come out and stay out."

"It helped me calm my temper down and discover myself. Now I'm more thoughtful."

"If someone believes in you, you don't want to let them down. And, you don't want to let yourself down."

"I feel like I must aim towards becoming a productive citizen.

There's a continuous flow of letters from inmates,
former inmates and their families. Slaughter has no
idea how many "thank you's" fill the files of the many
churches who sponsor inmates or parolees, but she is
sure they would also be substantial.

Even in a prison setting, good news travels far and
fast. Inmates in other facilities soon requested the
same benefits as those of Occoquan I and II. Prison systems in other areas from as far away as Nassau, Bahamas have shown an interest in what was done to help
inmates.

Volunteers are aware that the Spiritual Enrichment
Program and the Sponsorship Program lend themselves
to manipulation, particularly by a man who is trying to
impress upon others his worthiness for parole. During
imprisonment, volunteers encourage the inmates to
come to chapel for any reason; for once they are there,
they know they have a good chance to impress upon
them the real benefits of commitment to the program.
In the churches, the intent is to build ties that can help
a man overcome frustration and self-doubt, so he can
rebuild his own life.

*The publicity about the Spiritual Enrichment Pro-
gram has already reaped many benefits in increasing
community awareness about the problems of prisoners.* As this awareness grows, so does the program,
and so does the probability that its graduates will succeed in the community at large.

And so it is conceded that the administration was
given a program that gave inmates an alternative. It reduced inmates' idleness. The staff was relieved of pressure because the program inspired and motivated
inmates so highly that it nullified some of the negative
inclinations previously held by them. The inmates now
have new direction and insight about their lives.

Some now think more about where they would strive to position themselves upon their return to the community. Finally the community is benefiting by virtue of the fact that those men who have been spiritually nurtured have gained strength and skills with which to cope with the world outside.

CHAPTER VIII

"A Light At The End Of The Tunnel"

While it is too soon to perform long-term recidivism studies of Spiritual Enrichment graduates as opposed to those who did not participate in the program, there is much evidence that the program does work. *Every time a former inmate makes a better life for himself, he benefits the community.*

Recidivism, "a tendency to relapse into a previous condition or mode of behavior," continues with alarming frequency. Each year, thousands of men and women find themselves returning to prison or to jail.

In order for recidivism to occur, one must first be incarcerated. Secondly, he must be released to return to the community. Thirdly, there must be another offense which results in his return to the institution. The problem of recidivism, to be analyzed and evaluated, should be placed in a frame of reference. Variables which are pertinent to the matter of recidivism include the reality of a parole violation or the occurrence of a new offense. If both have occurred, then both factors are reviewed.

Participants in the final decision to reincarcerate an individual might include a staff member in a halfway house, the parole officer, a prosecuting attorney and a judge. *The reasons for recidivism cover a broad spectrum.* A man who commits a new robbery-murder offense would present a compelling reason for terminating his parole. Conversely, a man who was only minutes late returning to the halfway house for a non-frivolous cause would provide a questionable reason for the termination of his parole status. *In other words, the truly considered judgment as well as the "whim" of an individual will impact on the final decision which affects the recidivism rate.*

Recidivism, for far too many persons, is akin to going through a revolving door. There is action, but little or no progress. There are times when a man is returned to prison due to a job loss and failure to notify his parole officer. This constitutes a parole violation, but not a *new* crime.

A static or a fluctuating recidivism rate can be viewed as an index of the viability and effectiveness of a program. Preliminary information suggests that the combined effects of the chapel renovation program, the spiritual enrichment program and the follow-up activity of the EVOL Prison Ministry is having the desired result. *Those men who receive EVOL services seem to be surviving longer in the community without incurring new charges (violations).* Categorical claims are avoided at this time as the program is so new and a definitive mechanism for a full evaluation has not been structured. Thus far, all emphasis has been put on service to offenders. Of the hundreds of inmates with whom Mrs. Slaughter has worked personally, approximately eight reportedly have returned to prison. All of these were for drug-related causes. One young man recently telephoned her with an unusual request. At the prison and on the street, he said, he was too tempted by drugs. Because of his weakness, he asked to be sent to a Federal prison where he thought he would have no access to drugs.

EVOL (love-spelling reversed) is an incorporated, non-profit, spiritually-based, bible centered ministry designed to improve the quality of life for inmates. It is predicated upon love for mankind with the hope that inmates will be motivated to become greater assets both to themselves and to the community. The main purpose is to help alter the dehumanizing effects of, and to eliminate some of the causes of recidivism. Experience shows that *for tens of thousands of men and women, imprisonment is tantamount to "warehousing." Human beings, while confined, often spend critical years of their lives in unproductive ways. With disturbing frequency, the net result is wasted human life.*

"An evolutionary process" generally describes how EVOL was formed. The initial effort involved the formation of an inmate's choir. Then it was reasoned that for a more optimal effect, a chapel renovation was an appropriate adjunct to forming a choir. Before long, Bernice began contacting individual ministers requesting that they provide religious services. Sooner than anticipated, she was pressured with details attendant to scheduling. Another few weeks slipped by when she conceived the idea of forming a ministry which could assist in handling the myriad details.

Another idea was tested: that was to program two services in the evenings, one immediately following the other. This, too, proved infeasible due to the administrative problems involved in the movement of so many men in such a short time span. Another practical problem was that it was physically draining on a minister to deliver two sermons so close together in one evening. Unfortunately the EVOL Prison Ministry had not grown sufficiently to provide more than one minister in a single evening.

It was realized that residents had multiple motives in coming to the chapel services. Their reasons included seeking individual help with their personal problems. Perhaps the presence of female volunteers was an added attraction. As time passed, it became clear that there was a demand for many more volunteers to assist if there were to be a "dent" in addressing the problems of inmates. This, then, led to recruitment of more, genuinely interested persons to carry on the work of the EVOL Prison Ministry.

The scope of EVOL's service is intentionally broad. This seems appropriate as *the gaps in assistance require a comprehensive approach to alleviating inmates' problems.* Anything short of that type of plan would appear to be futile. Experience is strongly indicating that certain services are needed *prior* to a person's release. There is frequent need for continuation of services for a period beyond the release date. EVOL's aim is to be realistically supportive without fostering unnecessary dependency upon the support system. Throughout the "helping process," volunteers must maintain their focus on the long-range goal—spiritual and emotional growth.

Services are divided into those which are provided *within* the institution and those which are provided *outside* the institution. This does not presuppose a clear dichotomy of services, as some are ongoing. For convenience, they will be listed as *pre-release* and *post-release* outreach services.

SERVICES RENDERED

Pre-Release	*Post-Release*
- Spiritual Enrichment series provided by ministers and their congregates	- Employment assistance
	- Financial assistance

SERVICES RENDERED (CONT'D)

Pre-Release	*Post-Release*
- Bible Study	- Shoes and clothing
- Spiritual counseling provided by interdenominational ministers	- Carfare to job until paid wages
	- Representation in court
- Counseling by lay people	- Counseling by telephone and in person
- Legal referrals	- Assistance in obtaining lodgings
- Providing shoes and clothing	- Crisis assistance in family matters
- Small stipends for services rendered in the chapel	- Medical and dental assistance
	- Sponsorship by churches
- Small allowances to certain residents to purchase items of need	- Providing food for families
	- Financial assistance
	- Providing job training assistance
- Receiving collect telephone calls from residents	- Encouraging men to satisfactorily meet their parole obligations
- Limited medical and dental assistance	- Counseling in specific matters
- Letters to the Parole Board on behalf of selected inmates	

SERVICES RENDERED (CONT'D)

Pre-Release	*Post-Release*

- Assistance to families in emergencies such as when death occurs.

- Contacting social agencies regarding the status of residents' families

- Maintaining a clothing bank

- Sponsorship by churches

- Pen pals relationships provided

Though EVOL Prison Ministry was founded as an "ad hoc" group in July 1985, incorporation was not accomplished until May 1986. During the entire 10 months of its unincorporated status, EVOL did not enjoy the benefits of a government grant or corporate financing. The services it rendered were financed through "out-of-the-pocket" funding by volunteer members of the ministry, often at considerable sacrifice. This imposed very real limits on what could be done. Now that incorporation is a *fait accompli,* it will solicit contributions to enhance future efforts. (An organizational chart appears in the appendix.)

EVOL regularly holds full membership meetings. On these occasions, experiences are shared (as well as by telephone). Members discuss the voluminous problems involving the residents as well as those men who are released. From the beginning, they recognized the need for coordinated efforts to avoid duplication of effort. This helped to reduce unhealthy manipulation of which some individuals are capable when seeking help.

In spite of the formidable obstacles that faced the volunteers, there were some rewarding bright spots. *The appreciation and the participation of so many men made the efforts seem totally worthwhile.* An added incentive arises from the fact that men served by the EVOL Prison Ministry tend to survive longer in the community. The recidivism rates for these men is significantly diminished, it is believed.

"Commendations"

"When I was in prison you visited me."

Mrs. Slaughter was well aware that prisons are not only in the United States but everywhere. While vacationing in Nassau, Bahamas she welcomed the opportunity to visit "Her Majesty's Prison."

Her Majesty's Prison is located on approximately 41 acres in Nassau, Bahamas. It is the only prison in the Bahamas. Men and women are sent there by boat or plane from lock-ups in other parts of the Bahamas.

The population of the prison consists of a few more than 1000 persons, situated in five different institutions: (1) Maximum Security, (2) Minimum, (3) First Offenders, (4) Female Department, and (5) Detention Center.

Mrs. Slaughter was quite amazed at the outside appearance of the prison. The buildings consisted of exterior stucco walls, which is characteristic of building material used on the island. She noticed the absence of

Photo by Bechet

At Occoquan, Bernice pauses to talk with a troubled, weeping inmate.

high walls, guards in overhead towers and high barbed wire fences. Instead, there was a low brick wall about shoulder high with twin iron gates over which a person could climb. The gates were only secured by a padlock. It did not look as if it were constructed to keep anyone in.

Mrs. Slaughter later learned that prison escape did not present a problem presumably because the island is small and there seems to be few places for a person to hide.

Bernice visits Her Majesty's Prisons, Nassau, Bahamas

She was escorted inside by neatly-attired correctional officers. Their well-tailored beige military-type uniforms resembled gabardine. Contributing to their well-groomed appearance were the highly polished shoes, the neat scarf-like neckwear and the caps with visors. One could easily imagine that *esprit de corps* (pride) existed among the prison staff.

One could sense a mutual bond between the officers and inmates. The officers appeared to have a genuine concern for the inmates' well-being. As a result of this, the inmates showed a high level of respect for the officers.

Mrs. Slaughter also talked to the (Bahamian) officials. She was assured by them that her desired approach to prison reform was in harmony with the Bahamian philosophy. They also discussed the Bahamian inmates' choir and how they actually go out periodically to perform in the community. She hopes to witness the same for the inmates choir at Occoquan.

Superintendent Donald Scott, aware of Mrs. Slaughter's endeavors, remarked: "Bahamians are spiritually inclined. *It is most important to help inmates spiritually.* If you want to get through life in a meaningful way, you can't leave God out. Satan plays with anybody's mind—that's why you have inmates. You have to know that Jesus is still in prison. When a fellow falls in prison, you have to help him know that Jesus has not put him down. You are forgiven and made pure if you know Jesus—All you have to do is to just ask Him and you'll be forgiven."

One would hardly recognize this as being a prison when passing it. For it is devoid of the impersonality of many prisons. "A dangerous environment doesn't readily change an inmate," says Supt. Scott.

"Our choir performs in various places in the community. As many as 50 inmates attend. Twenty-two are choir members and the others assist in setting the stage for carrying out other necessary tasks in preparation for the performances," concluded Scott.

When leaving Mrs. Slaughter thanked them for the courtesy they had shown her. The invitation to return to the prison was cordially extended.

News of the chapel project is receiving not only local, but national and international attention. Commendations and plaques issued locally are listed below: (copies of the documents are included in the Appendix).

1. Letter from President Ronald Reagan, dated October 10, 1985.
2. Proclamation from Washington, D.C. Mayor, Marion Barry, proclaiming Friday, October 11, 1985 as BERNICE B. SLAUGHTER APPRECIATION DAY.
3. Letter from Congressman Walter E. Fauntroy, House of Representatives, Congress of the United States, dated October 11, 1985.
4. Letter of Greetings from David A. Clarke, Chairman, Council of the District of Columbia, dated October 11, 1985.
5. Letter from Dr. Calvin W. Rolark, President, United Black Fund, Inc., of Greater Washington, D.C., dated October 11, 1985. This letter advised of $1500.00 pledge toward the Chapel Renovation Project.
6. Bernice is prominently featured in the 1985 Fiscal Year Annual Report of the D.C. Department of Corrections.
7. Council of the District of Columbia Resolution No. 6–323, dated October 8, 1985. "The Bernice B. Slaughter Recognition Resolution of 1985" Section 2 of the Resolution states that "The Council of the District of Columbia recognized the outstanding dedication and leadership of Bernice B. Slaughter in bringing to fruition a project which will continue to have a positive impact on the lives of prison inmates for years to come."

Plaques Received

1. On April 22, 1986, Mrs. Slaughter became the seventh person, since 1960, to receive the Bureau of Rehabilitation, Inc.'s G. Howland Shaw Award for outstanding community service. Standing with her were eight former inmates of Occoquan. Their convictions had included, robbery, assault and drug use, but all were now gainfully employed.

2. A plaque was presented by James F. Palmer, Director, D.C. Department of Corrections, for outstanding contributions to the religious community of Occoquan Correctional Facility I and II, 1985.

Media Coverage

1. The Washington Post, July 6, 1985; Essence Magazine, January 1986; Afro-American Newspaper, June 1, 1985; Potomac News, Woodbridge, Virginia, May 30, 1985 and June 24, 1985; Jet Magazine, August 5, 1985 and Message Magazine, November 1986.

2. She was interviewed by various television shows: Channel 20, "Eyes on Washington," June 10, 1985; Washington, D.C.'s Channel 9 (WDVM) "Capital Edition," June 23, 1985, produced a documentary highlighting the innovative achievements of this project.

3. On August 11, 1985, CBS World News aired the interview they had with Bernice, concerning this project. Cable News Network aired the project on Sunday, August 18, 1985. She was interviewed on WYCB Radio Station's "Soundoff" on Thursday, August 21, 1985, February 27 and July 10, 1986. The German TV Network (ARD) filmed on August 30, 1985. That interview highlighted moments of her efforts. She was interviewed by Mal

Johnson, Cox Broadcasting, on October 3 and by Rhonda Kinchlo, WTOP Radio, on October 4, 1985.

One quickly realizes that the various plaques and commendations merely acknowledge what has been accomplished. In terms of what yet remains to be done, the successes are similar to an initial footprint in what hopefully will become a well-worn path.

In the foregoing story, there has been a detailed account of what one woman has done. An evaluation of that work is timely and a brief review of the sequence of events is offered. During her recovery from her ailment, this woman expressed a desire to turn an "inconvenience" into an opportunity. Using her extraordinary talent, versatility, resourcefulness, courage and zest for life, she inspired others to join her and to support her efforts to provide special benefits for prisoners. Her inspired leadership quickly won the support and dedication of the inmates themselves.

The prisoners, practically without exception, felt rejuvenated by the attention *they* received and *by their own participation.* For the first time, some of the residents found themselves captivated by a special personality, sparking their involvement in a notable project. Along with elevated spirits, *there was some behavior modification along desired paths.* Community involvement has become more intensely focused on Occoquan Facilities I and II. *Men released from the institution are finding it easier to survive the transitional period as a consequence of the very personal supportive services they receive.*

The manner in which the whole endeavor proceeded illustrates a method which succeeded and which holds significant promise. It can serve as a successfully tested model for other communities. This person-to-person, voluntary and comprehensive approach seems to be an effective tool for combatting recidivism and promoting rehabilitation.

Dedication has a cost which cannot be evaluated in monetary terms. Synonymous with commitment, it is a quality or trait that emanates from within an individual. It possibly reflects society's values and standards as interpreted by the individual himself. That quality mirrors a person's self-image, needs, goals and life view. Could one expect to find firm dedication apart from specific goals and values?

There were, however, a number of difficulties attached to the kind of success achieved and the level of involvement required. For instance, volunteers sensed attitudes which they interpreted as a *generalized unreadiness,* on the part of the department, to accept their approach to helping inmates. They were inclined to wonder if what they interpreted as opposition was not intended to frustrate and defeat their efforts. *Were those efforts seen as threatening to traditional practices and beliefs?*

Also counted among the difficulties was the wave of requests for service which inundated the volunteers. Slaughter noticed increasing demands upon her time and limited energy. At points she reached a state of exhaustion.

Among the problems was opportunistic individuals who attempted to use the volunteer effort for their own political gain. A case in point was a minister who wanted to take charge of the project in order to recruit the inmates for his personal political organization. When he was not permitted to do this, he spoke negatively of the effort in a ministers' conference. He did not want the conference to support the pew fund raising effort. Thankfully, his effort was not successful.

The price of dedication includes the loss of privacy, anonymity, and some inconvenience. Expectedly, there was some personal expense to the volunteers as there was no operating budget.

"What Others Can Do"

The progression attained in this chapel renovation effort, as well as the Spiritual Enrichment Program, demanded extreme sacrifice. And for those who will now offer themselves to the continuing effort, there will be the necessity for similar willingness to sacrifice.

"I'm excited and thrilled about your project. You are doing so much good. What can I do to help?" This is a typical response to the discovery of the Occoquan effort; and the answer is that every well-meaning citizen can do something beneficial. Some of the challenges are to help persons *to know just what it is they can do and where and how* their involvement may begin.

For example, heavier emphasis should be placed on crime prevention, reducing recidivism and on rehabilitation of offenders. It is assumed that, finally, interested persons can best decide what it is they can do. They will have to assess their circumstances, goals, resources and priorities. A multi-pronged approach to the problems mentioned above, for convenience of discussion, can be considered in parts.

Prisoners themselves have a particular interest in working on their problems. They have the invaluable commodities of time and energy to devote to problem solving. They probably could benefit by capable persons who can help them to direct and to coordinate their efforts. Prisoners might be considered the *primary* beneficiaries of the efforts that are made. The *secondary* beneficiaries may be the community, since it appears to be impossible to help prisoners without helping society at the same time. *Incarcerees, collectively, comprise a rich source of knowledge, experience and wisdom regarding what probably can and should be done.* Prisoners have had opportunities to reflect while in confinement and to gain new perspectives on their life situations. They have had opportunities to share with other prisoners what probably has gone wrong in their lives. There is a collective wisdom that ought not to be overlooked. When considering that some may have developed psychological problems, they do, however, have ideas of value to express.

They can help to formulate proposals and programs. They can petition top level directors of prison systems, state governors, state legislatures, and even the Legislative Branch of the Federal Government. In addition, they can petition the President of the United States requesting funds for educational, recreational and vocational training programs, with therapeutic results as the main objective.

Volunteers can be a priceless resource for helping to carry out the objectives of a well-conceived, coordinated and comprehensive program. The fact that they are volunteers, if carefully selected and supervised, suggests that they will bring to the task the intangible quality of real, personal concern that can reach inmates on a very basic level. Volunteers function in much the same manner as the "Big Brother" or "Big Sister" organization. One volunteer, for example, can sponsor several inmates. The number has to be carefully regulated as one individual (resident or ex-offender) can need much support. The time and resources of the volunteer also must be carefully considered. There should be supervision of the volunteers as there are many pitfalls that can be encountered. No one individual, no matter how intelligent or how mature, knows all of the answers.

Volunteers can recruit more volunteers. They should be screened and given an opportunity to go through a carefully structured orientation program. They can develop a handbook for volunteers. Coordinating services and sharing experiences is indispensable to the ongoing nature of the volunteer work.

It is conceivable that regular training sessions would be valuable and that new volunteers would be added. In addition, an ongoing assessment of work and procedures will be valuable. These sessions could stress many things such as standards for effective volunteerism. Non-paid staff need to be fully aware of the type of setting in which they are operating. All need to be aware of the special needs of prisoners: attention, service, communication, casework services and the need to be open, firm and honest with them. Although many prisoners are well-practiced in the art of manipulation and "conning," they are not helped by indiscriminate and irresponsible manipulation. It is essential that honesty and respect be indispensable parts of the working relationships.

Volunteers, of course, *must coordinate* their services with prison officials and other prison staff. *Volunteer staff would not replace prison staff, but provide the ancillary services which prison staff cannot adequately provide.* A volunteer pool ought to be an unlimited resource. The many can go a long way toward addressing the multiplicity of problems experienced by inmates and their families.

In the orientation of volunteers, pertinent institutional rules, regulations, policies and procedures can be taught. Again, it is emphasized that volunteers *do not replace* prison staff, but merely assist in carrying out rehabilitative measures.

Schools on all levels are potential resources to address the problems of incarceration, recidivism and rehabilitation. School faculties and the students, themselves, on all levels, can do effective things to promote a comprehensive plan. For instance, as a preventive measure, even elementary school children can be better informed about the need to seek help with their own problems. Parents, too, can be better educated about what can and needs to be done. Little children can stage plays and skits which will put them in role-playing situations where they are required to think and to make "important decisions." Students also can create posters, write letters and petitions to governing bodies requesting that more be done to prevent crime. They too often are victims and even perpetrators. This possibly sounds naive, but the people who are affected by adverse social phenomena should be more constructively involved in applying solutions to their problems.

The support of schools is construed to mean *all levels of education.* Valuable resources, may be found on every level. Therefore, the sophistication of the efforts would vary with the educational rank. Each campus organization conceivably would have something specific and desirable to contribute. This includes time, ideas, effort and funding. The funding, though, just might require special funding-raising projects.

Civic organizations often are powerful resources in dealing with the problem of crime prevention, serving the incarcerated, reducing recidivism and fostering rehabilitation. *It should be remembered that sound rehabilitative measures can help to appreciably diminish recidivism.*

Chambers of commerce throughout the Nation have an interest in measures taken to improve conditions in our communities. They, too, can be strong allies. They can be helpful in determining their roles in solving the problems alluded to in the above paragraph.

Teacher associations on all political and jurisdictional levels probably can be enlisted to assist in the development of a national movement.

Other professional organizations, of which there are many, can and do make valuable contributions. Exploratory efforts should be made to get professional organizations to underwrite scholarships with stipends for prisoners, parolees and probationers who meet sound and equitable standards of motivation, conduct and achievement. This just might prove to be a very positive reinforcement to individuals who need it.

Law enforcement organizations on all levels perhaps can be more effectively "wired in" on a comprehensive national approach. What could possibly be the effect of scholarships underwritten by individual police officers as members of organizations? Could it be that unusually tough problems require unusually conceived methods in working toward solutions?

NATIONAL CRIME PREVENTION AND REHABILITATION WEEK is March 1-7, 1987. *Though this is fictional and speculative at this time, it does not have to remain so.* This can become a reality if the President of the United States would proclaim it. Executives of state, county and municipal governments can support this action with proclamations for their particular jurisdictions. This possibility merits exploration as quickly as possible. A high priority needs to be established. How appropriate that it would be established by the highest executive office in the land.

Individual congregations and church conferences throughout the Nation can lend inestimable, but energetic support to a movement that literally would benefit the entire Nation. Again, the individual congregations and church conferences can decide in just what direction their thrusts would be aimed. It would be wonderful if they would deliberate on the matter of

scholarships and stipends as incentives as supportive
measures.

*Foundations, Industrial Organizations, Manufac-
turers and Corporations* are sources that should be
queried on the matter of providing assistance for offenders. Might it be that such moves could help to alter
the thinking of inmates?

The media has an enormous contribution to make.
The millions of people who are reached through the various mediums would be exposed to a massive educational and appeal program. There are the newspapers,
magazines, television, advertisements on train, bus,
airport and boat terminals that would help to increase
exposure. They could even sponsor national essay con-
tests to win support.

Other prison ministries. Other prison ministries
could join in a coordinated national movement. Radio
and television ministries have an excellent opportunity
to promote the national well-being by including more
outreach services to aid rehabilitation efforts.

PREVENTION. Prevention can be addressed at all
the levels mentioned above. The suggestions merely list
ideas that can be considered and are in no way thought
to be conclusive or exhaustive.

What yet needs to be done. Heads of various national and local organizations should be brought together in a conference to pool their collective thinking
about how to segment and to deal with the problems
mentioned above. Perhaps March 1987 *could* be the
month in which this could be done. Symbolically the
spring season is an auspicious time to begin something
new.

Re-entry centers for men returning to the community are in short supply. For the individuals who need
this type facility (half-way houses), their adjustment
can be enhanced during the transitional period between
the institution and the community. All reasonable efforts must be made to keep the centers *drug free.* Urine

surveillance just might be mandatory as an objective yardstick to determine the degree of abstinence that exists. The re-entry centers should have staff counselors available for emergencies and as a continuing service. The re-entry centers should be maintained, to the highest practicable degree, with resident labor.

Prison choirs. Choirs, where feasible, should be permitted to perform at various community functions. This includes churches, convention centers, public and private schools, college campuses and other appropriate places. Logistical problems certainly will be anticipated, but they alone should not preclude the implementation of this kind of expanded activity. It is recognized that permission for ventures would have to be obtained from the top level of the political office having decision-making authority. Certain risks would be inherent in this type undertaking. But it can be a viable rehabilitative tool.

Employment. In that employment is such a fundamental factor in a person's adjustment, an improved, stronger network of employment services must be worked out with employers, including city, county, state and the Federal Government. More of the ex-offenders can be screened for service with the armed forces.

Changing attitudes. Attitudes toward our prison population requires a general overhaul. There are so many salvageable people who languish in prisons. Some men are there for frivolous reasons, and other alternatives might be more appropriate and efficacious. Here is where the *Proclamation of National Crime Prevention and Rehabilitation Week* could prove to be more beneficial. It would attach a higher level of importance which can help to reduce the negativity toward the general prison population. *The prisons are full of people who need help.*

"Blurbs from Inmates"

The following letters received by mail are published as written. Names and identification numbers have been changed to protect the identity of the inmates, with their knowledge and consent.

So many times we hear nothing because we don't really listen. Sure, we may sit politely and quietly while someone is speaking, but our minds have raced to the next item on the list that we wish to discuss. While smiling and nodding the head in agreement with what is being said, we are miles from the topic of discussion, anxiously waiting for the speaker to finish so we can begin.

But the cry is heard by one who really listens, not with just the ears, but also the mind, the eyes and the heart. And once the cry is heard, a good listener's task is not completed until he finds a way to stop the cry, ease the pain and make the conditions better.

A key factor in the success of Mrs. Slaughter and the EVOL Prison Ministry is their ability to listen. They listened to inmates who had problems with other charges pending in other states. They listened to others who were concerned because they had no family or outside support. They listened to inmates that were drug users and needed unavailable medical attention to conquer the problem, while other inmates were afraid of being raped or killed while in prison. They listened to those who seemingly made a mockery of religion and to others who obviously didn't believe in anything or anyone. They listened to scared men who were scheduled for release and had no place to stay, no job, no money, and no clothes to wear once they "hit" the streets. Where could they possibly go but back to Occoquan?

After Mrs. Slaughter and the EVOL Prison Ministry heard the cry, they found ways to make conditions better. Many of the inmates now had a new song to sing, and members of the ministry could listen to their songs. They listened to families, churches and community organizations that were supporting their loved ones, while drug users were now receiving available medical attention. They listened to men who had jobs, places to stay and clothes to wear once they were released. For many of the inmates, this was the first time that they felt someone really cared about them and their situation.

Everyone at one time or another has something to say. This also includes those who were incarcerated. You may ask, what could they say to me? But more importantly, would you be willing to listen? Would you be willing to find a way to stop the cry, to ease the pain, to make conditions better?

A considerable number of residents express themselves in written form. So let us look and try to experience the agonies, feel the loneliness, the bitterness, the frustration, and degradation. Let us also acknowledge the warm glow of love, peace and hopes for a better tomorrow as they share themselves with us through "Blurbs from Inmates."

To Mrs. Bernice Slaughter,

I am a resident of Occoquan I, located in Lorton, Virginia. I'm writing this letter just to let you know what I

expected once I was incarcerated and what I hope for
once released to society.

I'm a native Washingtonian born and raised in a
family of six with two deceased sisters and without a
father. I was raised in a decent christian household. Being the youngest of the family I was never exposed to
much of life's problems and vital situations. I also lived
on a mapped life-style such as school, work after school
(which lead to an average of B varied grade average),
worked around our church and attended Sunday morn-
ings.

I loved sport activities, but when I was fifteen years
old I had two vital accidents with my upper legs and
was hospitalized for one-third of a year with a tutor at
home. I didn't miss any school acceleration and completed school successfully.

I was nineteen years old when I smoked a joint,
drank a beer and even attended my first party. This is
the point in my life when I strayed from my mother's
wing. In the meantime I was introduced to "Jeannie" a
female in college (1st year). I must have been the best or
at least close to the best thing that ever happened to
her because she's still here. But as time carried on I
was forced to leave my apartment and come back to
D.C. That's when I couldn't get a job paying enough to
continue making my car and apartment payments. I
needed money to keep my health and strength.

Soon I came in touch with a cousin that lived in the
"fast lane." So I indulged with drugs heavier than ever.
Where as I came in touch with various types but always
kept my values that I will never erase such as going as
far as injecting drugs. Not realizing I was deep in that
type of life-style as I was, I was stage 2 hooked, not
stage 4 or 5. When I say stage 2, I mean using almost
everything except ingesting pills.

Finally, I was arrested then incarcerated. Once I was
incarcerated I felt like for what I was caught with
wasn't worth all the time I received. Especially after be-

ing in a drug program for eight months out of a twelve month program and still received the same amount of time I would have received if I had stayed incarcerated.

Boy-oh-boy I'm extremely bitter now, but after reaching my maximum limit of bitterness I finally came down to realize what was I to do now? My problems were how it was in Lorton? I had no idea what it was like after seeing hundreds of Black males continuously talking about not "Lorton" but "Lawton" for slang or illiterately speaking. I wondered would I be jumped by several giant hard-core criminals and raped? Would I be stabbed for being green, not knowing the jailhouse ropes or will I get visitors with support. All of everything came upon my thoughts.

But once I came to Occoquan about eleven days later I heard an announcement come across the dormitory saying "If there's anyone who's interested in choir practice go to the chapel!" I did go to the chapel that day which looked like an abandoned building where as soon as I returned to the dorm it was a must that I take a shower because this was the dirtiest place on the compound. That day I got to meet this woman that taught us new-comers gospel music. This was the same day I notice another woman moving around the chapel and she always introduced herself with her husband. But by just constantly returning to the chapel on certain dates the piano ladies Ms. Barnes and Mrs. Slaughter returned.

My worries and problems began to wither away, like a candle with a flame to it—slowly but surely. Once I began letting myself relax by hearing and singing new or familiar hymns on the piano which almost bring tears to your eyes. When I heard them, I reflected back to my church experience before I smelled my pi—! Finally everything was being pieced together. A schedule on a daily basis—school, exercise, and choir practice. Before this time I worried about my life in prison and now I feel extremely secure by having someone "real" here in prison.

As time passed I continued to make picture frames out of cigarette paper wrappers to past time away. But again she helped me by offering to help sell my hand-crafted picture frames and I couldn't refuse her offer. This was getting too good to be true. But the best is yet to come for everyone.

Now the chapel is almost completed and we have chapel services with fiery outside guest ministers with their choirs, ceremonies with Occoquan's very well disciplined choir and a resentful prison chaplain. He feels intimidated by a miracle which had started to shake-up all Occoquan's residents' soul with the tremendous portion of God's Word and works being applied to a spiritually dead overpopulated prison. She has helped me financially when I was broke, mentally when I was confused and physically when I was not healthy. Mrs. Slaughter has freed a lot of people here along with myself. Now people here are more peaceful among each other. Also she has helped so many men here worry less about their loved ones on the outside and inside. Mrs. Slaughter is similar to Harriet Tubman, but not "steala-way" but "help and peace along the way."

I think it was so beautiful to bring in the community to see all the Black men and bring us hope to strive for a better life.

I really think that Occoquan I & II is really in a bad situation as far as living conditions, food, and medical care. If the administration was to constantly let our D.C. area congregations continue to come in our little community then our government would be criticized about Black men being treated like animals here. The outsiders would pursue the facts of high taxes in D.C., while their sons are treated like misfits. Or they would pursue a number of issues concerning Occoquan Facilities, most of all the well-being of the Washington area's scarce number of Black males.

Many nights I wonder what can I do to repay her for what she has done for me? All I can come up with the help of God is being faithful to her to the best of my ability with all my heart. And that's the God's honest truth!

Sincerely,

Mr. Faith Ful
D.C. #234—56

To Mother Bernice Slaughter, Whom I Love so dearly,

How are you doing? Fine I hope. I'm doing just fine thank you. I would like to take this time out to express my deepest feelings towards you. But first of all I truly hope that when this letter reaches your destination it will find you and the EVOL Prison Ministry in the very best of health mentally, physically and most of all spiritually. Mrs. Slaughter I want you to know that I sincerely love you from the bottom of my heart and I need you to help me with a very serious problem.

I'm also writing you this letter because I'm in the need of a place to stay. Mrs. Slaughter I want to talk with you as if you were my mother one-on-one because I feel that I can open up to you and tell what's on my mind. You see when I was coming up I really didn't get the love a child would expect from his mother and stepfather. My father died when I was eight years old and he was a very caring person. Mother Slaughter, whenever I come back out there in that productive society I want to prove to myself that I can be a responsible citizen, but all I ask is that I love and be loved by others. And that's one of the elements missing in my life.

I sincerely hope that you will understand what I'm saying and take this letter into consideration and thank you for your cooperation. May the grace of God be with you and your family through all trials and tribulations and may he also add a blessing to your life. Amen.

I would appreciate it very much if you would send me a $5.00 money order so that I can get cosmetics. It would be highly appreciated of you Mother Slaughter.

God loves you and so do I.

Yours truly,

Mr. Love Less
D.C. #345–67

Dear Sister Slaughter,

I want to express my deepest appreciation and thanks to you and EVOL for your concern and involvement in helping us both in and out of this "dungeon of despair."

As you know, the term "dungeon of despair" doesn't begin to describe the hell we must suffer in dealing with this situation. I thank God for you and EVOL and people like you who care enough to get involved and try to do something about it.

This is not to say that we are all innocent or that the majority of us should not be incarcerated, but I am saying that we can't be treated like animals and be expected to act like human beings. We should not be made to trade our humanism for animalism just to survive the conditions maintained and condoned by the very people who put us here for supposed wrong doings.

If I sound angry, it's because I am. I'm hurt and surprised. Angry because I can't be my own man. Hurt because in order to get free and stay free I must become their boy. Surprised that the public has been duped into believing that the criminal justice system works. And what's worse is that even if they have no concerns about us, they don't care enough about their money to look and see that the monster they are fighting is the monster that they are paying to create.

Anyway, I thank you and EVOL for all you've done and may God through Christ Jesus, ever bless you.

Mr. Bit Ter
D.C. #789–45

Dear Mrs. Slaughter,

I pray when this letter reaches you, you will still be doing God's work. I also want you to know this may be the hardest letter I am going to write.

In this letter, I will try to help you understand how I got here, and what my life has been like since I started to use drugs. My reasons for using drugs is because I was young, foolish, and wanted to know what life was about. After ten years of pain and living lower than most animals, I have come to understand my life don't have to be like it is at this point. I am sure this letter won't come close to what I want to say about how my life has been, or I also understand that my fears and pain can't be put on paper. Most important, I understand at this point and time in my life, if I don't get some real help, I know I'll die from drugs.

My last three years (as you know) I was supposed to be getting some help, at the same time being off the street down Occoquan. The help I am talking about is for my drug problem. That's really one of the biggest jokes I've been a part of. Occoquan has just as many drugs as 14th and W Street! *I really never had a fighting chance.* I am weak for dope and when I was sent down there the court knew that fact. What I think maybe the court didn't know was that I would be going nowhere I could really have a chance to make it and stay clean. Occoquan is not the place for me, or anyone with a drug problem.

At the same time, I want you to know I've been to two drug programs before I came to Occoquan (Second Genesis and Last Chance), both was in an area filled with dope.

Maybe I need to get away from Washington. At the same time I need you to help me get this message across to whomever, so I really can get some help. I need your love and understanding more than I ever will at this point and time in my life.

Please try to understand. I will die without your help.

Keep praying for me,

Mr. Hate-My-self
D.C. #220–00

Dear Mrs. Bernice Slaughter,

There is so much happening today that contradicts yesterday; yet today will contradict tomorrow.

I am going to attempt to place and express my innerself within those words that I am going to write. Also this is the second letter that I am writing. The first one came back.

Mrs. Slaughter, upon coming back to this warehouse of human suffering and seeing you again, I asked you not to give up on me. And you replied: "My friend, how can I give up on one of my boys?" Through those few words you said to me "you cared." And to a person such as me, it means the world.

Society is being cheated of its tax dollars. There is so much that could be done that could alleviate recidivism, drug addiction as well as violence within prisons. Yet we constantly hear from Mayors, city council members, as well as tax payers, "build more prisons," yet no one wants a prison in his back yard, so look out when the space shuttle program resumes again. The priority may be prisons in outer space.

As I look back, I can remember furlough programs, college furloughs, and employment-seeking furloughs, but because, let's say five (5) out of a hundred messed up, all of these positive programs have been brought to an end. These were positive programs which afforded individuals, who would have never thought of higher education, the opportunity to obtain it.

My problems have never been addressed by the Department of Corrections or the Bureau of Prisons. My first adult incarceration was at the age of 18 and I am now 39. I will be 40 in two months. Throughout this period of time, and at no point was I free. I was introduced to drugs in Lorton in 1965, and I haven't been able to be drug-free over an extended period of time. I don't even understand myself at this point. Within the warehouse there is no one to turn to. I am not per se placing the blame on anyone, but what I am saying is: where have I had time or the chance to take control over my own life in society? Maybe this is debatable.

Yet I have goals as well as desires. I would like to own my own business (home improvement). I would like to learn to drive, dance and find the perfect woman. But most of all, I would like to become champion over my drug and alcohol addiction.

I sometimes wonder whether I am destined to always be imprisoned or what? This question revolves around my ability to adhere to rules and laws of this abnormal society. I don't have to make major decisions, I don't have to worry about when or where my next meal comes from, and I know I have a bed to sleep in each night. I have some times wondered if I'm allergic to people because I get great enjoyment out of being by myself. I find that I am most happy working by myself. I feel very uncomfortable trying to interact with others.

I would like to point out that I have a mother and I love her very much. So much so that when in jail, I never worry her about helping me in any way.

Well, Mrs. Slaughter, I hope you can understand

what I am saying. And also I want you to know God loves you and so do the guys down here.

Love,

Mr. Seek N. Self
D.C. #000-24

Dear Mrs. Slaughter,

I thank God to be able to write to find out just how you and your organization are feeling. Quite naturally, I hope you all are at the best of God's loving tender care.

As for myself, giving my thanks to God for letting me see and be healthy one day at a time. I'm programming over here very hard, going to school, working in the Culinary always keeping myself occupied to stay away from naught and confusion. As I'm stating, I have written you before, but I wish not to worry you too much because I know you have your own problems to sort out.

I'm just one man in need of a favor in which, I seem to be having problems with. And I seem to have no outside protection at this time. I'm a young man that has potential to do constructive things to benefit myself in society, but putting out my helping hand to help myself as well as others.

I have been doing some research on myself and now it has come to a point that I'm ready to show the real side of my life as "Mr. Potential." By the way I'm 25 years old and will be 26 on August 18.

This world I'm living in is just not meant for a man of my motivation and determination. After all, every good man can take a fall or two before waking up. (Now I really see daylight.)

In my case I've been incarcerated for approximately 3 years of my precious life. Now I'm able to look to the future because the past has nothing to offer. So I must be positive and move right along with my life.

So you see I can use my smarts to become successful in this world. Mainly, I'm a businessman. A man with such knowledge should be in society paying his dues to show the community that he or she is reliable and dependable to do anything that there is to be done to better themselves.

Getting directly to my main point, asking a question straight from the heart! Will you be able to help me with the charge in Laplata, Maryland, Charles County Court? I really do need some help so that I can stop worrying my Mother as well as myself. After all, mentally I'm really hurt deep down inside, and can use all the help I can get from a friend.

Oh! The parole board has given me 9 months here at Youth Center II. I'm down to 8 months now. I really do depend on you giving all the helping hand that you can and I know you will do anything you can to help me.

Because you are very special to me and the world, what I say to you is not for you to help me, it's just straight from the heart.

When I first saw you I had already accepted you as my second Mom, but I never had a chance to talk with you. I have your phone number but there's been a few problems, I've run out of cash since being incarcerated. If possible, could you send me some pastors of your church organization so we can talk. Because over here the religion is not anywhere as beautiful as yours.

By the way I haven't been to court in Laplata, Maryland yet. But they have a detainer on me. If you could investigate for me I really would appreciate it. The reason I don't call is because we know my position but hopefully it will be alright one day soon. With God's help I'll overcome all these problems.

Sincerely yours,

Mr. Potential
D.C. #123–45

Dear Mrs. Slaughter,

I'm writing this letter in effort to thank you for the opportunity to participate in your program and to thank you for your undying concern. When I first came to you I needed someone to give me a chance and be on my side, but to my surprise, you were much more than that. You were instrumental in helping me make parole and got me a job that I enjoyed. The transition back into society was not an easy one for me, but you were there to assist me spiritually, morally, financially, and even let me come live with you until I got on my feet. I'm really glad that you let me stay with you and now I realize that if I stayed with you a little longer, I probably wouldn't be back in the position we first met. It's really unfortunate that I returned to prison because you gave me the tools I needed to function positively in society and gave me a chance to grow. Your disappointment in me is matched by my own because I owe much more to myself and to you. At this point I'm beginning a sentence of 5 months to 3 years with a parole eligibility date of December 2, 1986. I ask that your prayers be with me and that I be able to continue participating in your program. I just enrolled in U.D.C. and I'm trying to stay mentally, spiritually, and physically active. I would like to use this time to best prepare myself to come out and be the productive person I know I should and can be. Again, I will need help in making the transition back into society and ask that the program assist me in any way that it can. Before closing I would like to again thank you and express my gratitude. For your human compassion, your undying efforts, and unselfish love you have given me. I have grown to love you like a mother and being one of your boys, I know it's over due time to get and keep some order in my life. May God bless and keep you.

Love,

KK
D.C. #89–100

Hello, Mrs. Slaughter,

It's my pleasure to first and foremost greet you in the name of God, the Father and our Lord Christ Jesus.

I believe I should do well to introduce myself at this point. Well, my name is "Thankful". I'm from Washington, D.C. and at present I'm here in a Federal Correctional Institution in New York.

Through one of the good brothers here with me, Mr. "Fine Person," I've learned somewhat of you, and the good work that you are a part of through the E.V.O.L. Prison Ministry.

Honestly, Mrs. Slaughter, I don't know why I'm writing per se. I've no specific reason. However, I would like to commend you in your work of love towards those of us whom many others have counted unworthy of love. Thank God he never felt that way and is a merciful and forgiving God.

"Fine" has shared how you ministered to him and to countless others down in Virginia; and oftentimes folk take other folk for granted, unfortunately. However, I practice and now through the grace of God find joy in being one of those who bring and offer rays of encouragement to those folk such as yourself.

So may the God and Father of our Lord Christ Jesus be with you and continue to bless and prosper you and the ministry there, now and always.

In Christ Jesus' Name,

Mr. Thankful
FCI 000—000

Dear Bernice,

My hope is that when you receive these lines you will be doing well, perfectly, you and your husband and family.

Bernice, I am sending this letter to let you know that I am very grateful for your attention and for your interest in helping not only me, but all of those whom you have assisted.

Listen Bernice, let me tell you, particularly, that you are more than a sister to me; you are a second mother, because as you know, my mother is in Cuba. I have faith that you will endure for many more years because God blesses you. God knows that you have a kind, generous heart, you are sweet, patient and you listen to all that he directs toward you. Women like you are hard to find.

Bernice, I am very pleased that I could see you past Friday; and I would like to continue seeing you. As you know, I know no one else to help me. All day long do I think about how to resolve my predicament. I would like to see my grandfather, but you know that I have no means to communicate with him.

I hope that all goes well. Write to me as soon as you receive my letter. I can read English but I cannot write in English. Give my regards to your mother, father, husband and children.

I will say goodbye now; I hope you have a good, peaceful day. I will never forget you. May God bless you forever. I love you.

Mr. Im Mi Grant
D.C. #075—47

Author's note: This spanish speaking inmate worked well in the chapel project. English speaking inmates enjoyed helping him to communicate. He is visited frequently by EVOL, PM.

Translation of this communication by David James Jackson, EVOL Prison Ministry.

CHAPTER XII

Why Grown Men Cry

Crying, for humans, can be considered nature's safety valve. *Perhaps not all cries are visibly tearful.* Could it be that at times they take the form of other behavior which might appear bizarre? Very often cries take the form of self-directed aggression, aggression against other individuals or against property. Often their cries express intense, intolerable, even excruciating pain. If this behavior is clearly understood, it may convey a distinct message—help me!

People cry for different reasons and under different circumstances. A list of possible reasons is offered below. Perhaps individuals will find several with which they can identify:

Grown men cry because they are frustrated.
Grown men cry because they are lonely.
Grown men cry because they are anxious and fearful.
Grown men cry because they are angry at themselves and at others.

*Grown men cry because they do not feel
     respected.*
Grown men cry because they are treated unfairly.
*Grown men cry when they are denied that which
     is rightfully theirs.*
*Grown men cry when they feel guilty about
     wrongs they've done.*
Grown men cry when they cannot say "I'm sorry."
*Grown men cry when they feel their manhood is
     threatened.*
*Grown men cry when they are spiritually
     bankrupt.*
*Grown men cry when they cannot forgive
     themselves and others.*
Grown men cry when they feel inadequate.
*Grown men cry when they cannot adequately
     express their feelings.*
Grown men cry when they feel misunderstood.
Grown men cry when they lack courage.
*Grown men cry when they cannot provide for their
     families.*
*Grown men cry when they feel physical and
     emotional pain.*
*Grown men cry when they are addicted to drugs
     and alcohol.*
Grown men cry when they feel they are failures.
Grown men cry when they lose their loved ones.
***GROWN MEN CRY BECAUSE THEY ARE
     HUMAN!***

Now, from inmates themselves, will you hear why
grown men cry?

Dear Mrs. Slaughter:

As usual I sincerely hope this letter finds you physically and spiritually sound. I'm well, but I find that I'm

trying to deal with so many feelings. Most of the time I'm feeling lonely because I am just that. Being surrounded by 500 other inmates does nothing for the void I feel within because there's no one here that I really know or trust. I'm lonely because my freedom has been taken away from me along with my family, loved ones, and friends who I need and who need me. I guess I'm stuck with loneliness in this time of separation—incarceration because I have no desire to exploit others to escape this misery. I will use this time to look into myself and learn from being alone because I know that I must endure.

I don't want to be here though and feel that I have been punished enough. Sometimes I feel so frustrated and find that I have a great deal to be frustrated about. I'm angry at myself to begin with for placing myself in this situation. I never gave myself a chance to channel my energy and intellect in a positive manner. This makes me want to kick myself because I know that I have the potential to be a productive and viable person within society. Being confined here seems to breed frustration because there's really nothing to do and the fact that it's terribly overcrowded. I mean we're literally walking over one another and this is potentially dangerous when it's hot, boring and there's no means of positive release. As a matter of fact the burning incident which took place at Occoquan I & II was a result of this I do believe. I'll never forget that evening because tension was extremely high here at Occoquan III and I got into bed to avoid any confusion. I didn't fall asleep, I was just laying there when I heard someone shout out "they're burning over there." I jumped up and ran into the pool room where I had an excellent view of the blaze which began to illuminate the sky. Soon blazes were popping up all over I & II and everybody at this facility was up. They were either at the windows watching the fire or they were by their beds packing their belongings just in case. I suddenly began to feel a real sense of fear because I didn't know what was going to happen here, but I was going to be ready and I prepared myself for the worst. Other than a few isolated incidents we got through it without much happening here but there was an overwhelming sentiment of pleasure that it had happened and a strong possibility of an outbreak occuring here. There's still a possibility of something serious happening and I'm extremely anxious to get through this incarceration period without incident. I'm anxious about regaining my freedom, putting my problems behind me, and begin to deal positively with the ones I'm sure to face. For now, I will continue to pray for wisdom, strength, patience, faith, love, peace, happiness, guidance, and freedom. My prayers are as always with you and yours.

May God bless you and keep you.

Love,

Mr. Had My Share
D.C. 831–00

Dear Mrs. Slaughter:

I would like to write you about things that make me cry. I have to say that at times I do feel lonely being locked down away from my family. I miss my wife and kids and I miss being in my church giving my worship unto the Lord. But only because I have Jesus on the inside of me am I able to handle the pressure. Sometimes I wonder if the guards down here or at the D.C. Jail go through a training process of how to treat inmates like dirt. They make it hard for a man that wants to make a change in his life. The only help that we get that if someone from the outside would put pressure on about the inmates. It seems like all the guards must get

together and say lets treat these guys like they are
never to be a part of society. They try to take your privi-
leges away from you. They make it hard for a person
that wants to make a change to do so. To be honest, if
most of them could, I believe that they would stop you
from using the bathroom. If you need them to do something for you it seems like it hurts them to do it. They
always pass the buck to the next shift in which you still
won't get what you need done.

Mr. Help Us
D.C. #859–57

Authors note: Is this an example of a rehabilitative
atmosphere?

Sunday, August 10, 1986

Hello Mrs. Slaughter,

I pray this little note comes and finds you and your
household in God's care and blessing. As for myself,
"praise be to God" I'm fine and well.

Please do find also with this letter, the "letter of
permission" you requested of me; it's my pleasure indeed.

I'd like to, at this time, thank you for accepting my
call and the rewarding conversation I received from
you. When the other call came in, not that I was eaves-
dropping, but I couldn't help overhearing it and I'm
honestly glad that I did. It made me reflect upon Mat-
thew 25: 31–40, and a story that I have based around
it. I want very much to share this with you. So I decided
that I should send it to you for your reading and just
ask that you shall return it to me. I pray it may bless

you with encouragement and even a word from God himself. Paul spoke of us encouraging one another in Romans 1: 11–12, 17.

However, you touched on a very profound truth; and that is, we, as God's own people, ought and need to learn to be Bible walkers instead of Bible talkers. Well, not *instead* of, but even more so, walking the talk. That heartfelt relationship with the Lord, not merely a head knowledge relationship. This is what I heard you "preaching" the other day, praise God, and it encouraged me.

I have much growing to do, and practice also (smile). There was a time that responsibility scared the heck out of me; I was afraid of failing. But praise be to God that there is no failure in him! And while I honestly don't know exactly what the Lord has for me, it came to me to just walk as he shall have me to do each day. Just doing that I'll be doing good (smile).

I thank God for the blessings he has provided me with along the way. And I somehow believe that to know you is gonna be one of those blessings.

God keep and bless you and yours, now and always.

In Jesus' name,

Mr. Will Endure
D.C. #000–01

Mr. "Will Endure" enclosed in his letter a verbatim expression from INVOLVEMENT: BEING A RESPONSIBLE CHRISTIAN IN A NON-CHRISTIAN SOCIETY. It appears in its entirety:

IF TRAVELERS on the Jerusalem-Jericho road were habitually beaten up, and habitually cared

for by Good Samaritans, the need for better laws
to eliminate armed robbery might well be overlooked. If road accidents keep occurring at a particular cross-roads, it is not more ambulances
that are needed, but the installation of traffic
lights to prevent accidents.

It is always good to feed the hungry; it is better
if possible to eradicate the causes of hunger. So
if we truly love our neighbors, and want to serve
them, our service may oblige us to take (or solicit) political action on their behalf. We shall not
just prattle and plan and pray, like that country
vicar to whom a homeless woman turned for
help, and who (doubtless sincerely, and because
he was busy and felt helpless) promised to pray
for her. She later wrote this poem and handed it
to a regional officer of a shelter:

I was hungry,
   and you formed a humanities group to discuss
   my hunger.
I was imprisoned,
   and you crept off quietly to your chapel and
   prayed for my reason.
I was naked,
   and in your mind you debated the morality of my
   appearance.
I was sick,
   and you knelt and thanked God for your health.
I was homeless,
   and you preached to me of the spiritual shelter of
   the love of God.
I was lonely,
   and you left me alone to pray for me.
You seem so holy, so close to God
   But I am still hungry—and lonely—and cold.

August 11, 1986

Dear Mrs. Slaughter,

This is one of your *adopted sons.* I use the word *adopted* in its full context because of the motherly, positive image you have become in my life. From the first time I met you, you have remained the same.

Mom, you have been a very positive motivation in my life. I can remember when I first came to Occoquan in the summer of "84". The place was a place for the ill-reputed, if you ask me. It seemed like there was no hope at all; and if there was any hope, it was hoping that you will get out of here alive.

All a man could do was lay around and think about the mess he has gotten himself in. As for me, I used to sometimes cry when I looked back on the things that I took my family and loved ones through. The times when I would call home and ask my father, who is poor, to try to get me bond money because I was locked up for stealing or selling drugs. The times I would leave my wife and kid home all alone for days and nights because I had to be with the fellows out on the corner. I used to cry when I would make a commitment to my loved ones to get into a drug program and clean up my act only to go right back to using drugs and hurting them again. I also remember the times I cried because no one would come to see me, or send me a few coins to get some of the small things I needed to make my stay here a little more comfortable.

Yes, I've had my share of crying, but now I do a different kind of crying. The tears that run from my eyes now are tears of joy. They are tears of joy because I know that I have someone in my corner that cares about all the tears I've shed; and that someone is Bernice Slaughter and the EVOL Prison Ministry.

They showed me that there is hope by giving me something I never thought I could get; they gave me spiritual growth. They showed me the way to Jesus Christ. They taught me how to sing a joyful noise to the Lord. All in all, they taught me how to live again through Jesus Christ; and since that time, I've been very happy. I might also mention that not only have I been happy, but my family and loved ones are happy also.

My family says they can hardly wait until I come home. They say they see a change in me that they never saw before. The so-called friends I used to have are not my friends anymore because they can't understand why I don't do the negative things I used to do. Mom, I really must say: you sure have made a real man out of your son and I am going to make you a real proud mother.

You know, I miss helping my father do things like working on his car; taking him shopping and helping him around the house. I miss things like taking my wife and kid to the parks and just sitting at home watching TV together. You know, I miss even little things like riding on a bus, going to the store and all the other things we take for granted when we are in the free world.

You know, Mom, I remember someone telling me that I will never amount to anything, but you gave me that something that I could be proud of; you gave me hope and you gave me love.

I love you and the other members of the EVOL Prison Ministry. Tell them all that I send my love and to keep up the magnificent work that God has chosen them to do.

P.S. who ever said that a man ain't supposed to cry?

Love ya!

Mr. Ready For Change
D.C. #111-11

August 11, 1986

Dear Mrs. Slaughter,

I'm writing to let you know how much I really appreciate working with you and being with you while staying in the Lorton Department of Corrections, correctional complex.

Mrs. Slaughter, before I met you, I was lost and didn't know what to do or who to go to. Before you and the EVOL Ministry came to the Occoquan Facility, I was lost. I couldn't see or be with my loved ones. My feeling was down so much and pressure on me, I couldn't do anything but cry. See, when a man comes into a place like this, he loses all of his rights. He can't do anything but put up with all the pressure from the inmates and the officers. I can't see my mother or father; that alone makes me cry. They are too old to come and see me. Every day this place is like hell. And the reason why is that a man does not have anything to extend his mind. He has nothing to grow on—no good programs for a man in here. If you want to see your Classification and Parole officer, you can't. They don't want to see you. If I had a problem and put in a request slip, the C & P officer will never call me or see me. Like I said, this place is like a mad house. Sometimes I feel like crying out loud, but I do not because I know that no one cares so I keep it all inside and it just keeps building up inside of me where I can't take any more. That's why I thank God for Mrs. Slaughter and the EVOL Ministry. I love you Mrs. Slaughter, you have been like my own mother. This place is designed for one reason—to keep a man going backward and forth, in and out. They can't do anything but come back because the jail can't offer them any job training. That's another reason I have to cry. With no vocational training, what can I do when I get out? I need a job and place to stay. I want to be with my kids. That's another reason why I have to cry. Being in jail is a very lonely time in a person's life and a very crying time. I need someone to talk to, someone who will understand me and love me and care for me. Without love, a person is lost. And that's what being in jail does to a person. It takes everything you ever had.

Yours truly,

Mr. Still Crying
D.C. #111–10
To my mother,
Mrs. Slaughter

August 12, 1986

Dear Mrs. Slaughter,

In a prison situation, a person has lots of reasons to emotionally want to cry. But due to the prison environment, a person has to be careful about not showing any signs of weakness such as crying. However, acknowledging the human factor that the Almighty has instilled in us, we who are in prison like to relate to our emotions and cry. We cry because we miss the normal things that any free person has access to. We miss our wives and children and not being able to provide for their needs. We miss our occupations, working with our minds and our hands to become productive members of a free society. It is a fact that the majority of incarcerated people are in prison due to their anti-social acts against society. Nevertheless, people that are in prison, in most cases, are highly intelligent and believe in their own intrinsic worth so much that we will cry in protest whenever we are denied the fundamental rights given to prisoners under the Constitution.

We cry because our potentialities are denied and are not permitted to grow. At the same time we acknowledge that our potentialities are a great deal better than anyone has ever permitted us to believe. We cry because we know that the development or improvement of the mind is only by education or training.

Most of the people in prison today will one day re-enter the society that put them away for their criminial activity. So I hope that the reformist on prison reformation have the fortitude to use these prisons as "development and training centers." God gives us many signs in creation. For example, life comes up out of an environment that is corrupt, but life does not accept corruption unto itself. The plant, the seed coming forth from mud and filth does not allow the filth to come into itself. When we eat the plant we don't eat the filth; we eat a clean life. We cry because we are in the prison environment everyday. Therefore, we don't want to become corrupt. Why do grown men cry? Because in prison survival is our number one priority.

Mr. Aware N. Stymied
D.C. #001—20

It is not unusual for Mrs. Slaughter and EVOL to appear in court on an inmates behalf if he has proven to be deserving. The ministry has been successful for the most part in getting favorable results for the inmate. We consider it important that a prison ministry would not only place emphasis on discussing the Bible, but more importantly carrying out the work of the Word. Attached is a capsule of the results of our appearance in court on behalf of the inmate whose letter is attached.

"Among EVOL's recent success stories is that of a young man who was charged with prison breach. It was

a difficult case because the defendant did not have a
defense and a favorable sentence was jeopardized due
to his prior criminal record. However, this young man
has gone through many changes since becoming an
EVOL member and so there was still hope. The organization worked closely and tirelessly with the defendant
and his attorney and these efforts paid off. After accepting an early plea of guilty to the charge, reviewing
letters of support from the organization, the defendant's family and his attorney, and hearing an allocution
by EVOL members Bernice Slaughter and Reverend Archie Griffin, which the prosecutor himself admitted
was "compelling and eloquent," the judge sentenced
the defendant to a term of probation. This victory
would not have been possible without the commitment
and hard work of all those who were involved in the
case. This young man has now been given the opportunity to become the fine citizen that all who have met
him know he has the potential to become."

Signed by the attorney in this case

Dear Mrs. Slaughter:

I hope this letter finds you in the best of God's loving care. As for myself, I'm living one day at a time. I
find it hard to believe I have committed my freedom
again by moving from prison to prison. When I came
back to prison, I didn't know where to begin because
my thoughts were confused; the inner mind was shut
out on thoughts about myself as well as my life. Then I
turned to God for some help. He lead me to some special
and outgoing people, Mrs. Bernice Slaughter and EVOL.
They were interested in helping people who were willing
to help themselves.

As I sit here incarcerated at D.C.D.C. putting my
thoughts about life together, a vision passed through

me. Being successful has always been one of my major issues in life. My purpose for being in this world was to help those who help themselves.

Being incarcerated is a sad case for me, because I have jeopardized my freedom which means so much to me. It takes only one wrong move and a man's whole life can go right down the drain. Being incarcerated is meant only for losers and I'm not a loser. I have always been a winner, but it has been a few years of bad luck.

Being locked in 24 hours a day, losing all contact with the outside world, having to be fed whenever they want you to eat, and locked in a room like a child for wrong doing is just not the way a man should live. These are open opinions about the jail lifestyle—not knowing when someone will just go crazy and stab or maybe kill you. Your life depends on you because the guards are never there when you're in need of help.

Jail life for me is the next step to death. If I could write a book daily about prison life many would read and take heed and never take the road of frustration, anger and humiliation, but you must be of the strong in this world of hell because the mind plays the biggest part of it all.

But there are some people concerned about their lives as I am. But they just don't have anyone to turn to. My advice to them is to ask God for forgiveness, repent your freedom and be sincere, and he will answer all your prayers. So you see I'm a man of great thoughts and hope one day to be a helpful citizen in the community. I really want to own my own business. I have been installing insulation for the past 8 years off and on. I will make it my business to put all effort towards fulfilling my dream of success.

(Back to prison life)

When my door shuts at night, I pray before lying down. The devil wishes to overcome the will of God. But

I have shut him down without a doubt because he has lead me into enough downfalls in life. So now I will become stronger and have faith in God. When your friends turn their backs on you, God will always be there. The way I feel about myself—kind, thoughtful, considerate, helpful, honest, loving, generous and appreciative for what I received in life.

Mrs. Slaughter, thanks to you and EVOL. You stayed beside me all the way. God will always bless all of you for what you've done for inmates. You are righteous to all. You are a friend to those who call on you. I must say you are most honest, careful, and the most outgoing people a human could ever have.

I'm really dissapointed that after all you and EVOL have done *it seems that the Occoquan facility is trying to replace your ministry.* But God will always answer prayer. People like you and EVOL should be a living legend across the world.

I can honestly say for myself when I get another chance in society, I promise this: never will I do anything to send me to prison ever again in my life. My life is too precious and valuable to just throw it away. I hope and pray that my family is staying in the word of God. To all, please don't get your life messed up, by even being around the wrong crowd.

P.S. Because of you, I'm always happy no matter what may happen.

Love You,

Mr. Lookin' Up
#003-30

Dear Mrs. Slaughter:

This is my feeling about my charge, conviction, sentence, and incarceration. First of all, I feel that my conviction is unfair. I was charged with assault with a dangerous weapon. I had been under attack, and, at the time, the weapons he (my attacker) was using against me seemed as dangerous as any weapons I could imagine. The man was much larger than me, and his weight and strength were a threat. I carry a knife in a belt case which I use as a box opener on my job. (I am a cook and I must open many boxes during the day.) After being struck repeatedly, I managed to relieve the knife from its case. I reacted to my attacker violently. I was found guilty, sentenced to two to six years and sent to Occoquan. I feel that I should not have been charged with assault since I did not initiate violence. My actions were a response to violence even though they were themselves equally violent. I should have been convicted of self-defense, but the District of Columbia has no provision in its laws for such a plea.

I became depressed and confused by the chain of events. I wondered over possible alternative actions. Even now I do not know of anything else I could have done to protect myself. I was sent to Occoquan Correctional Facility feeling more confused and mistreated than I have ever felt.

At Occoquan I had hoped to get a new skill or improve on an old skill. At the very least, I hoped to better myself in some way. When I arrived, I found myself among hundreds of discouraged disenchanted people like myself. I was in a prison that housed more than 1700 men who slept less than 18 inches apart. It had too few toilets, showers, and sinks. It did not have enough light, and there is no quiet place to think, write, or to find a moment of peace. I was in a prison where flies swarmed the restrooms, dining area, recreation areas, and sleeping quarters. I was in a filthy place; it was cruel and impersonal, a place with no positive stimuli, a place where self-improvement and rehabilitation cannot make it beyond the realm of thought alone.

At Occoquan, I have seen killers go free and an innocent man die in a riot. I watched correctional officers
shoot men after the riot had calmed, men who were sitting on the ground in submission. I have been lied to,
lied on, and forced to lie on the wet ground during a riot
in which I played no part. I have been forced through
smoke, tear gas, and falling bricks and then shot at. I
have seen men raped by other men. I have seen men
placed in segregation units and called "flashers" because female officers walked unannounced into their
sleeping quarters and found them naked, sometimes in
the process of changing clothes or preparing for a
shower. The injustices of D.C. justice is multi-furious.

I feel as though I have been placed in a time machine
and taken back 100 years or more in time to a place
with designs to tear down morales, values, and princi-
ples; to a place bent upon the ripping apart of relationships, a place which replaces what humanisms and
social attributes it destroys with a vast malevolent
void. (My family is gone now; my wife divorced me, and
I have lost my home to creditors). I have seen other
prisons, but none like this one. In most prisons there
are some unifying ideas left relative to "the American
Dream," a hope for freedom, God, and country; ideas of
love, family unity, and brotherhood; ideas necessary for
a sane and normal person and a sane and normal life.
No such ideas exists here. It is as though I have been
taken out into an ocean at midnight, dumped overboard
with the sharks, currents, and other seafaring hazards
and told to sink or swim. It is as though I have been
taken on one of John Barth's "Night Sea Journeys."

The only bright spot here is the Chapel. It is the
most beautiful and *only* bright spot, but even its light
is growing dim. I can feel it. The inhumaness is encrou-
ching in the church, and I can feel that the pressures
are frustrating its most loyal servants. *Soon it will be a
church in name only.*

Mrs. Slaughter, your efforts in creating a church served as the greatest unifying element we had. We will not forget your efforts in creating it for us. Whatever brightness remains is a monument to you. Whenever we see that beam of light, our collective consciousness will be illuminated with ultimate radiances.

Love,

Mr. Dis Gusted
D.C. #0?1–7?1

While one must be alert to manipulation, substantive communication is an important element in the rehabilitative process. It affords a sharing of ideas and feelings through several forms, oral, aural and written. Sensitivity to what is being expressed requires attentiveness and responsible concern. It is through the spiritual enrichment program at Occoquan that this concern has been manifested.

It is recognized that many requests are cries for "give me something to do."

CHAPTER XIII

Revelation

From the retrospective vantage point of a volunteer, this chapter, perhaps, is one of the most significant. It portrays the total experience of volunteers who labored in a facility controlled by the D.C. Department of Corrections. Although different prison facilities eventually became involved, the primary focal point is Occoquan Facilities I and II.

In October 1984, Bernice was introduced to a prison staff member of the Occoquan Facility by a family friend, Jaronza Ellis, for the purpose of organizing an inmates' choir. In the beginning, the volunteers were greeted with "red carpet" treatment. However, as success appeared inevitable, it seemed that suddenly the red carpet was subtly snatched from under their feet. The volunteers were left virtually prostrate on the hard floor of apparent rejection and opposition. It was thought by some that failure was hoped for, expected and even predicted. Perhaps the prophets of gloom and doom underestimated Bernice's resolve. She had a *raison d'etre*—a reason for being. Her reason for being was her desire to enrich the lives of the inmates through her musical talents. To quote Johann Friedrich Schiller, "Opposition always enflames the enthusiast, never converts him." She was not dissuaded; she had strong supporters.

Bernice's enthusiasm was quickly communicated to the inmates through her endeavors. Soon the men found themselves singing even while exiting the chapel following rehearsals. There was a carry-over of this activity even into the dormitories where correctional officers reported that they had sung far into the night. We would often hear from inmates and friendly staff that there were even fewer altercations among inmates. Some correctional staff reported that their jobs were made easier as a result of reduced tension in the dormitories.

Because of her own physical limitation, Mrs. Slaughter needed additional assistance in working with the inmates' choir. Within a short time, she had engaged the volunteer services of a talented musician and colleague, Mary Casey. Mary obviously enjoyed teaching the residents as they responded well to her instruction. However, after several weeks, Mary decided that she could not continue her work with the inmates. She could neither understand nor accept certain apparently negative attitudes of some members of the staff.

After Mary left, Bernice secured the services of Barbara Barnes, still another talented musical-choir director. The choir continued to progress in spite of a few troublesome administrative problems.

After a period of time, it became evident that serious problems existed relative to getting residents from the dormitories to the chapel for rehearsals. Frequently residents were not sent to the chapel on time. Residents claimed they often were not released from the dormitories for scheduled rehearsals. On many occasions, they arrived there just prior to "count time" and had to leave the chapel shortly afterwards for the head count.

A Cooperative Effort

Former Administrator Arthur Graves chats with Pastors Herbert A.
Schwandt and David James Jackson.

At other times, they arrived so closely to lunch time
that there was not sufficient time for rehearsals. Still,
many were willing to forego the meal. With disturbing
frequency, there was too little time for rehearsals, but
the strong motivation of those involved served to mini-
mize the negative effects.

The level of frustration was heightened when Ms.
Barnes, after traveling approximately 25 miles each
way, sometimes could not readily gain access to the
chapel. Her arrival was scheduled and therefore anticipated. Other volunteers experienced similar problems
and concluded this to be a pattern of rejection because
of its consistency. They found the following adage to be
true: "Stones and sticks are thrown only at fruit-
bearing trees." These are the words of D. Saddi. In ac-
cordance with that philosophy, the volunteers assumed

Photo by Bechet

Problem-solving conference in the Main Conference Room at Occo-quan Facilities I and II. Participants from left to right: former Administrator, Arthur Graves, guest minister, and Bernice B. Slaughter, with pastors David James Jackson, Herbert A. Schwandt, Arthur Preston and layman, James N. Slaughter, Jr.

that their efforts must have been effective. Otherwise there would have been no cause for opposition.

In an effort to resolve the difficulties, a group of volunteers met with Arthur Graves, the administrator at that time, to discuss possible solutions. They clearly outlined to him the discrepancies they found. Before any problems were satisfactorily resolved, he was transferred to another facility.

Still embued with the "the-show-must-go-on" attitude, the group continued to function through what it construed as obstructive tactics. They held several conferences with the new administrator, David Decatur. In each meeting they identified the recurring problems encountered in their work. The ad hoc group of volunteers who met with him became the nucleus of the EVOL (L-O-V-E) Prison Ministry, Inc.

The inmates claimed that, prior to the arrival of these volunteers, with the exception of the Muslim services, there was scarcely any religious participation. Responding to this void and to the inmates' request for more religious activity, Bernice scheduled Series 1 of the Spiritual Enrichment Program. This program was endorsed by EVOL and by the new administrator. The series involved participation by Bernice's psychologist, Dr. H.D. Johns, community ministers, their families and members of their congregations, gospel groups and even lay people who taught bible classes. Because of the tremendous response and acceptance by the residents who were truly inspired, Bernice responded to their request for Series II of the Spiritual Enrichment Program. Under this arrangement, the residents and the correctional staff knew far in advance things that were to transpire.

"Forgetting" her physical handicap (she labels it an "inconvenience"), she moved ahead with executing this plan with expertise and aplomb. There was a clamor among the inmates for more of the same inspirational services as they could see that she brought with her the love of Jesus Christ. To quote Bernice: "Who needs political power when you're inspired by the power of God, evidenced by the power of love and exemplified in the power of the cross of Jesus Christ. Without love, life is meaningless."

It appears that love and helpfulness are seen as a threat. As a result, jealousy and anger can be engendered. Despite these impediments, her work was not stymied. Nothing can remove the love in the hearts of the residents. The good that was done was incalculable.

Though optimism prevailed, it appeared that "passing the buck" was a tactic sometimes employed to keep the religious volunteers off balance and discouraged.

The evidence also suggests that generating confusion between volunteers and correctional staff was another tactic skillfully employed. There is reason to believe that this was attempted, too, in an effort to create dissension between residents and the volunteers. Could it be that chaos and confusion are prerequisites for functioning at this facility?

The tactics that the volunteers regard as negative are discouraging and emotionally draining. Still they are committed to helping the men that they started with in the program. They still desire to help to reduce the recidivism rate. The EVOL Prison Ministry desires to do constructive things; this is difficult enough without unnecessary obstacles.

EVOL is constantly faced with complaints from inmates about the overcrowding. In their posture they can only remain baffled. Extreme temperatures in the dormitories doubtlessly contribute to the mounting pressures on residents. And then, too, the lack of viable programs exacerbate the situation. Personal problems of the inmates seem too often unaddressed; they seem to feel that not enough interest is shown in their spiritual needs by staff and the community. Many inmates believe that the EVOL Prison Ministry is being forced out of the institution and that the main source of their community support is being denied them. Given this particular package of problems, the frustration and despair seems comprehensible.

Asked for her reflections on the project, Bernice remembered that in the beginning favorable comments were frequent. However, as the project progressed, compliments sometimes were replaced by insulting remarks. She remembers that early on, some staff were concerned about her well-being. For example from one she would hear: "Mrs. Slaughter, aren't you tired?" Her reply was: "At their insistence, the 'boys' made me a pallet of carpet and bricks so that I could rest." While some staff members apparently were pre-occupied with finding reasons to sabotage the effort, there were those staff members who were sympathetic and humane'', Slaughter reflected.

The negativism is in contrast to her having affectionately been assigned an honorary prison number: 000—444. This suggested acceptance of her effort by some. On the other hand there were comments such as: "She only did this for personal gain." Bernice scoffs at the suggestion as frivolous and inaccurate. It seems to pale in importance when one considers the incarcerees had reached a "dead end" in the institution. Their treadmill-type existence did nothing to improve their chances for successful living in the community. She also wonders if the persons making such comments would have refused her help had *they* been the incarcerees in identical circumstances.

In assessing the "personal gain" motive, she does see where there was some personal gain. She found more meaning in life—something that is uplifting and sustaining. Concurrently, she provided something of lasting value to the incarcerees. They found someone who was willing to take risks to improve the circumstances of their lives. One resident, responding to a disparaging remark said: "There never is a cause without a critic". Does this man have an "attitude for gratitude?"

In hindsight, one could get the impression that those staff members who genuinely found value in the project were relatively secure within themselves. The natural question arises: *What did opponents really have to fear?* Were their jobs threatened? Not at all. Their personal security was not threatened. Is there any reason they, too, should not have benefitted by improved circumstances?

In the final analysis, Bernice thanks God even more for surviving a heart attack at a crucial time in her life.

She feels that she is able to serve mankind from a much deeper and appreciative perspective.

A prison expert predicted that there was likely to be an eruption at Occoquan Prison. It occurred about one week later.

Early on the morning of July 10, 1986, the inmates seemingly gave expression to the accumulated pressures they felt. They apparently implemented a highly organized and systematic attempt to burn the dormitories. Television screens in thousands of homes were illuminated by images of a mighty conflagration—fires ignited by the seeds of discontent and further fueled by flammable materials of which the dormitories are constructed. Approximately 14 buildings were engulfed in flames, but the chapel was spared.

The D.C. Mayor, following the burning, made a televised address from the chapel. It seems that the chapel stands to serve all who need to use it. We can only hope that the persons in control of the institution will manage the administrative and human concerns with sufficient skill and care so that residents will never again feel the urge to resort to burning buildings. The chapel seems to stand as an oasis in the intense desert heat giving comfort to those in need. May the chapel forever stand as a potent symbol of love for all mankind. And may that love be accepted for the sake of spiritually enhancing aspirations of the residents.

Occoquan burned. The chapel still stands.

APPENDIX A

The Occoquan Prison Chapel Project was planned and executed by Bernice Brent Slaughter during January 4, 1985 and May 29, 1985.

The charts with labeled, numbered blocks indicate the general priorities assigned to each item during the renovation period. In some instances, several items received simultaneous attention.

Figure 1

1 piano	2 piano cover	3 ceiling & walls	4 ceiling panels	5 folding chairs
6 folding tables	7 bibles	8 vinyl for chairs	9 organ & cover	10 velour draperies
11 landscap- ing	12 song books	13 exterior painting	14 installa- tion of wooden cross	15 flood lights for ceiling
16 new doors	17 panic bar for door	18 new carpet	19 awning & canopy	20 candela- bras
21 pulpit & choir loft	22 fountain	23 changing directory	24 planters for walkway	25 plaques honoring donors

APPENDIX B

Under the Spiritual Enrichment Program Series, there was a pronounced increase in activity that benefitted residents. The calendars for the months of July through December 1985 reflect the increase in that activity.

Figure 2
Calendar For July 1985

* = Number of residents attending   EM = EVOL minister
X = Community church & minister   G = Guest minister

Testing The Effectiveness Of The Spiritual Enrichment Program						
SUNDAY	MONDAY	TUESDAY	WEDNESDAY	THURSDAY	FRIDAY	SATURDAY
	1	2	3	4	5	6
7	8	9	10	11	12	13
14	15	16	17 7: 30 PM X * 76	18	19	20
21	22	23	24	25	26	27
28 7:30 PM X * 59	29	30	31			
Two activities scheduled.						

APPENDIX B

Figure 3

Calendar For August 1985

* = Number of residents attending   EM = EVOL minister
X = Community church & minister   G = Guest minister
B = Bible study   GP = Gospel program

| Testing The Effectiveness Of The Spiritual Enrichment Program |||||||
SUNDAY	MONDAY	TUESDAY	WEDNESDAY	THURSDAY	FRIDAY	SATURDAY
				1	2	3 Gospel program * 122
4	5	6	7 B * 78	8	9	10 Gospel program * 84
11	12	13	14 X * 100	15	16	17 EM * 200
18	19	20	21 B * 80	22	23	24 X * 85
25	26	27	28 X 7:30 PM * 93	29 ARD German TV network * 100	30	31 X & male chorus * 98
Ten activities were scheduled.						

APPENDIX B

Figure 4

Calendar For September 1985

* = Number of residents attending   G = Guest minister

X = Community church & minister   GP = Gospel program

EM = EVOL minister   B = Bible study

Testing The Effectiveness Of The Spiritual Enrichment Program						
SUNDAY	MONDAY	TUESDAY	WEDNESDAY	THURSDAY	FRIDAY	SATURDAY
1	2	3	4 X * 98	5	6	7 guest psycholo- gist * 100
8 GP *137	9	10	11 G * 83	12	13	14 GP * 160
15	16	17	18 X * 170	19	20	21 EM * 63
22 X * 180	23	24	25 G B * 71	26	27	28 EM * 185
29	30					
Ten activities were scheduled.						

APPENDIX B

Figure 5

Calendar For October 1985

* = Number of residents attending   EM = EVOL minister

X = Community church & minister   G = Guest minister

B = Bible study   GP = Gospel program

Testing The Effectiveness Of The Spiritual Enrichment Program						
SUNDAY	MONDAY	TUESDAY	WEDNESDAY	THURSDAY	FRIDAY	SATURDAY
			2 X * 109	3	4	5 prayer & praise session * 82
6 X * 86	7	8	9 G B * 73	10	11	12 EM * 173
13 X * 86	14	15	16 EM * 143	17	18	19 X * 127
20 X * 94	21	22	23 X & chapel quartette * 91	24	25	26 GP * 81
27 X * 156	28	29	30 X & Chapel quartette * 97			
13 activities were scheduled.						

APPENDIX B

Figure 6

Calendar For November 1985

* = Number of residents attending   EM = EVOL minister

X = Community church & minister   G = Guest minister

B = Bible study

Testing the Effectiveness Of The Spiritual Enrichment Program						
SUNDAY	MONDAY	TUESDAY	WEDNESDAY	THURSDAY	FRIDAY	SATURDAY
					1	2 Prayer & praise * 67
3	4	5	6 EM RE: employment * 133	7	8	9 Prayer service quartette * 75
10 X * 93	11 X * 84	12	13 (guest) * 62	14	15	16 gospel concert * 145
17 X * 105	18	19	20 X * 168	21	22	23
24 X * 87	25 X & cha- pel quartette	26	27 EM * 136	28 X 10:30 AM	29	30 X & chorale * 162
15 activities were scheduled.						

APPENDIX B

Figure 7

Calendar For December 1985

* = Number of residents attending   G = Guest minister

X = Community church & minister   EM = EVOL minister

Testing The Effectiveness Of The Spiritual Enrichment Program						
SUNDAY	MONDAY	TUESDAY	WEDNESDAY	THURSDAY	FRIDAY	SATURDAY
1 10:30 AM EM * 110 7:30 PM X * 68	2	3	4 G & cha- pel quartette	5	6 10:30 – 3:00 in- dividual counsel- ing	7 G * 89
8 10:30 AM EM * 115	9 7:00 PM X * 74	10	11 7:00 PM bible study * 78	12	13 2:00 PM individual counseling	14 X & choir * 103
15 10:30 AM EM 7:00 PM X * 63	16	17	18 EM * 120	19	20	21 Wintley Phipps Concert *425 (in gym)
22 10:30 AM EM * 103 G * 76	23 7:00 PM Candle- light Service * 79	24	25 10:30 AM X * 82	26	27	28 7:00 PM EM * 104
29 10:30 AM EM * 77 7:00 PM X * 68	30 X * 84					
23 activities scheduled						

APPENDIX C

Appendix C contains some samples of forms that are used in the EVOL Prison Ministry.

Figure 8

Dear Pastor John Doe:

Thank you for accepting the invitation to appear under the Spiritual Enrichment Program Series at the Occoquan Facilities I and II Chapel. The inmates have been informed of your consent to serve them and anxiously await your presence.

We look forword to seeing you on _____ at _____.

Please be advised that you should return the attached form to me within (5) five days of the above date.

Sincerely,

Bernice B. Slaughter
Religious Volunteer

Enclosure
BBS/gt

Figure 9

INSTITUTIONAL ACCESS FORM FOR RELIGIOUS SERVICES

This communication is prepared to request institutional access for the purpose of rendering religious services on _____, _____ at _____.

Everyone on this list will be active participants in this service for the residents (inmates).

Name   Address

_____

_____

_____

_____

_____

_____

_____

_____

_____

_____

_____

_____

_____

_____

_____

Signed: _____ Date: _____

Figure 10

EVOL PRISON MINISTRY, INC.

Part 1 of 2   (Part 1 For Resident)
                        Please Print

                                        ID #_____
                                        Dorm #_____
Name_____Age_____Date_____
Home Address_____
City_____State_____Zip Code_____
Repeat Offender? ☐ Yes   ☐ No (If yes, list charges and
dates on the back of this form)
Charges For This Offence_____How long?____Parole Date____
Nearest Relative's Name_____Relation_____
Address_____
City_____State_____Zip Code_____
Telephone #_____Married ☐Yes ☐No Children ☐Yes ☐No
Education Level_____Job Skills_____
Religious Preference_____Hobbies_____
Reason For This Interview_____
_____
_____

_____

Part 2 of 2   (Part 2 For EVOL Counselor)

Name_____
                            Figure 10 (Cont'd)
Location_____Date_____Time_____
Area of Discussion: _____
_____
Assigned to: _____Date_____
_____
_____
Special Concerns: _____
Disposition: _____
Follow-Up: _____
Remarks: _____
_____
_____
_____
_____

Figure 10A

Washington, D.C.

Towards the end of a significant impact upon society, EVOL has engaged in a rehabilitation effort that has resulted in a recidivism rate of noteworthy reduction for the ex-offenders.

EVOL Volunteer Profile

The EVOL members include:

Bernice Slaughter, retired congressional aide

James Slaughter, retired social worker

David James Jackson, minister, United Methodist Church

Herbert Schwandt, pastor, Lutheran Church

Maizie Sellers, mortician

Janis Allen, secretary, Pentagon

Arthur Preston, pastor, Baptist Church

Earl Day, Sr., pastor, Community Church

Consuelo Gantt, elementary teacher

Edward Gantt, retired NASA employee

Archie Griffin, associate pastor, Baptist Church and Admin. Assistant, Dept. Agriculture

Juanita Griffin, homemaker

LaVerne Dickerson, secretary

Robert Owens, associate minister, Pentacostal church & program analyst

Barbara Bowen, U.S. Postal employee

Alice Young, order processor

The EVOL members volunteer as little as one hour and as much as 24 hours a day of their time! With no set time limit for any specific area or service for the inmates, each EVOL member volunteers his/her service to an area in need of attention.

Although the EVOL members fulfill diverse roles in the community, each member has the following characteristics in common:

(1) a genuine concern for the overall well-being of each offender and released offender by giving encouragement, attention, and most of all, love

(2) a desire to bridge the gap between the community and the institution

(3) a desire to bridge the gap between the community and the offender, as well as the ex-offender

(4) a desire to bridge the gap between the offender and the institution, by way of the community

(5) a willingness to initiate vital programs, including
    spiritual
    self-awareness (counseling)
    employment

The motto of EVOL is **"The word (of God) interpreted through profound service."**

For information write to:

EVOL Prison Ministry, Inc.
c/o 3016 P Street, S.E.
Washington, D.C. 20020

WHAT IS EVOL?

EVOL (Every Volunteer of Love), is a non-profit organization founded in July, 1985. It originated with the efforts of Bernice B. Slaughter, who initially wanted to volunteer her musical talents by forming an inmate's choir at the Occoquan Facilities, I and II. After visiting the institution, she decided that there was an even greater need to refurbish the 1915 aged, dilapidated chapel. After soliciting over $40,000 from the community, (both private and religious sectors), she drove 64 miles a day from her home in Largo, Maryland to the Lorton, Virginia institution to deliver the materials needed to complete this project. Accompanied and assisted by her husband, James, Bernice shared her vision with approximately 16 talented inmates of the institution. Ranging from painters to welders, the inmates helped reconstruct the chapel under the guidance of this small-figured, heart attack victim. After completing this miraculous project within a period of only five months, services of many kinds are rendered for the inmates, sponsored under both EVOL and other organizations.

Though not funded in any manner by organizations (neither private nor governmental), EVOL has been providing the following services since its existence:

Within the Institution

- Spiritual enrichment series brought by various members of the community
- bible study sessions
- spiritual counseling
- legal referrals
- clothing, food, medical and financial assistance for inmates and their families
- collect calls for any reason at any location
- court appearances on behalf of the inmates (citing attendance and characteristics noted by EVOL representatives)
- allowances for cleaning the chapel
- assistance to deceased family members of inmates

Within the Community

- court appearances on behalf of the released offenders (citing attendance and characteristics noted by EVOL representatives)
- clothing, food, medical and financial assistance to ex-offenders and their families
- legal referrals
- employment services including (1) counseling (2) referrals
- spiritual counseling
- transportation
- shelter
- collect calls for any reason at any location
- visits
- job-training assistance
- sponsorship by churches
- maintenance of clothing bank
- providing of letters to parole boards, etc.

APPENDIX D

The information presented below is an excerpt from the D. C. Department of Corrections Annual Report for Fiscal Year 1985.

Figure 11

Occoquan Facilities I and II are part of a complex of eight different institutions administered by the D. C. Department of Corrections.

The Occoquan Facility was opened in March 1982 to house misdemeanant residents. In December 1983, Occoquan was divided into two separate institutions. Occoquan I housed felons and Occoquan II housed misdemeanants. Presently Occoquan I has a capacity of 436 and houses adult felons while Occoquan II has a capacity of 450 and houses Youth Act cases and Adult Diagnostic males. The Record Office staff processed approximately 12,000 resident movements in and out of the facilities during fiscal year 1985.

Occoquan I and II Facilities

Population

Black Males	98.2%
Age Group 21—30	65.8%
Single	82.5%
H. S. Education	34.7%
Unemployed	48.5%
Crime Index Offenses	41.1%
Drug Offenses	32.7%
Drug History	25.0%

APPENDIX E

This section pertains to the commendations that were issued recognizing the accomplishments at Occoquan Facilities I and II.

THE WHITE HOUSE

WASHINGTON

October 10, 1985

Dear Mrs. Slaughter:

I understand there's going to be a "Golden Celebration"
at Occoquan Prison on Friday, marking the completion
of the chapel project, and that you very rightly are to
be honored as the prime mover, and principal architect.
Congratulations!

You and those who helped you deserve every credit.
I especially want to commend all those who rolled up
their sleeves and just kept going till the job was fin-
ished. When they look around the chapel and see
what they have accomplished, they will always feel a
sense of pride.

You saw a need and you went ahead and met it. This
is the spirit that has made America great, and a great
place to live. I want to send my sincere thanks, and
Nancy joins me in this.

One last thing: keep up the good work!

Sincerely,

Ronald Reagan

Mrs. Bernice B. Slaughter

WALTER E. FAUNTROY
DISTRICT OF COLUMBIA

REPLY TO

WASHINGTON OFFICE:
☐ 2135 RAYBURN HOUSE OFFICE BUILDING
WASHINGTON, D.C. 20515
(202) 225–8050

DISTRICT OFFICE:
☐ 2041 MARTIN LUTHER KING, JR. AVE., S.E.
SUITE 311
WASHINGTON, D.C. 20020
(202) 426–2530

Congress of the United States
House of Representatives
Washington, D.C. 20515

COMMITTEES:
DISTRICT OF COLUMBIA
SUBCOMMITTEE:
CHAIRMAN, FISCAL AFFAIRS
AND HEALTH

COMMITTEE ON BANKING, FINANCE
AND URBAN AFFAIRS
SUBCOMMITTEE:
CHAIRMAN, DOMESTIC MONETARY
POLICY

SELECT COMMITTEE ON NARCOTICS
ABUSE AND CONTROL

October 11, 1985

Mrs. Bernice B. Slaughter
Religious Volunteer Coordinator
Occoquan Prison Chapel Renovation
 Project

Dear Mrs. Slaughter:

It is with sincere appreciation that I write to commend you for your commitment and dedication to the Occoquan Prison Chapel Renovation Project. You have single-handedly taken on this project to raise the funds needed for the construction of pews for the Interfaith Chapel.

Yours is a ministry of love reflecting an unwaivering determination to enhance the environment wherein the residents of Occoquan I and II assemble to hear the "Good News" of the Gospel.

On this special occasion, the dedication of pews celebrating the completion of the Occoquan I and II Prison Chapel Project, it is only fitting that we look to Christ who reached out and embraced those in all walks of life, the poor man, the rich man, the thief and the priest.

I am certain that the work you have begun at Occoquan will bear fruit as the lives of men are changed for the better. The new pews in the Interfaith Chapel will be a place where they can experience the joy and peace of worshipping our Lord.

As the representative from the District of Columbia in the U.S. Congress, please allow me to express the gratitude of all our citizens for your selfless contribution.

May God continue to bless your prison ministry and may the inmates at the Occoquan Facilities I and II use the Interfaith Chapel as a place to commune with their Creator and fellowship with each other.

Sincerely,

WALTER E. FAUNTROY
Member of Congress

OF GREATER WASHINGTON, DC

1625 EYE STREET, N.W.
SUITE 903
WASHINGTON, D.C. 20006
(202) 822-9116

Dr. Calvin W. Rolark
President

Dr. Philip J. Rutledge
Chairman of the Board

October 11, 1985

Ms. Bernice B. Slaughter
Coordinator
Occoquan Prison Chapel Project

Dear Ms. Slaughter:

Please be advised that the United Black Fund
is pledging $1500.00 to your noteworthy
project.

Our community is most fortunate to have
people like yourself, people interested
in providing the emotional support and
guidance necessary for human growth and
development.

For information regarding allocation of
the $1500.00 you may contact Mr. Rupert Bond,
Comptoller, United Black Fund, at 822-9116.

Very truly yours,

Dr. Calvin W. Rolark
President

CWR/dlp

COUNCIL OF THE DISTRICT OF COLUMBIA

WASHINGTON, D.C. 20004

DAVID A. CLARKE
Chairman

GREETINGS FROM CHAIRMAN DAVID A. CLARKE
COUNCIL OF THE DISTRICT OF COLUMBIA

OCTOBER 11, 1985

Dear Friends:

As Chairman of the Council of the District of Columbia, it is my pleasure to extend sincere congratulations to those whose dedication and hard work have brought to fruition this ceremony recognizing the culmination of the "Golden Hour" and the dedication of pews for the Prison Chapel Project at Occoquan facilities 1 and 2. I especially wish to extend deep thanks and appreciation to Ms. Bernice B. Slaughter for all of her efforts on behalf of this project.

I am certain that the residents, staff and officials of Occoquan 1 and 2 greatly appreciate the financial support and unselfish human effort which has been contributed to enhance the spiritual health and growth of the resident population.

Without the commitment of volunteers such as Ms. Slaughter many goals that are set, particularly for that part of our citizenry that is usually considered outcast, may not ever be realized.

I know I speak for the citizens of the District of Columbia in wishing you well, and expressing our hope that the Prison Chapel Project at Occoquan will continue to offer opportunities of spiritual growth to the resident population.

Sincerely,

Dave Clarke

Figure 16

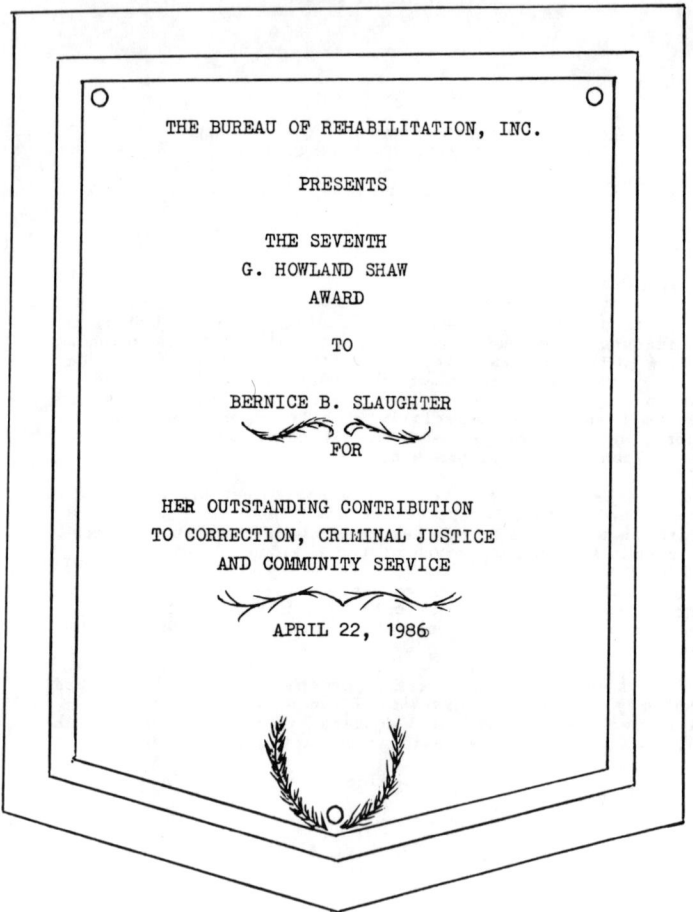

THE BUREAU OF REHABILITATION, INC.

PRESENTS

THE SEVENTH
G. HOWLAND SHAW
AWARD

TO

BERNICE B. SLAUGHTER

FOR

HER OUTSTANDING CONTRIBUTION
TO CORRECTION, CRIMINAL JUSTICE
AND COMMUNITY SERVICE

APRIL 22, 1986

Program

Presiding .... Mary D. Braxton, President, Board of Directors
and Editorial Director, WJLA-TV (Channel 7)

Invocation .... Reverend McMacoy Edwards, Associate Minister,
Bible Way Temple Headquarters, Washington, D.C.
and Bureau Volunteer

Opening Remarks .... Mary D. Braxton

Staff, Volunteer and
Foster Parent
Recognition .... Harry A. Manley, Executive Director

Presentation of
G. Howland Shaw Award
to
Bernice B. Slaughter .... Mary D. Braxton

Vocal Solo
"I Give You My Life" ......Whitley Phipps

Keynote Address .... Frank Smith, Jr., D.C. Councilmember, Ward 1

Benediction. .... Reverend McMacoy Edwards

Music by Bill Osborne

1986 Banquet Committee
Rachael Lowder, Co-Chairperson
William Wooten, Co-Chairperson
Vickie Henderson-Zegar
Sondra Hyman
Joseph Matelis
Jake Matthews
Charles McDougle
Victor Sterling
Coletta Barbee, Staff
Cecelia Cunilio, Staff
Harry A. Manley, Staff
Walter Tabory, Staff

*56th Anniversary Banquet
(1930-1986)
of the*

Bureau of Rehabilitation, Inc.

BUREAU OF
REHABILITATION INC

*April 22, 1986
Fort McNair Officers Club
Washington, DC*

JOIN US AS WE CELEBRATE 56 YEARS
OF CLIENT-BASED SERVICES FOR THE
CRIMINAL JUSTICE SYSTEM AND
HONOR THE SPECIAL MEN AND
WOMEN WHO ARE WORKING TO
MAKE A DIFFERENCE.

Mary D. Braxton, WJLA-TV . . . *Mistress of*
    and Board President   *Ceremonies*

Frank Smith, Jr., ... *Keynote Speaker*
    D.C. Councilperson, Ward 1

Bernice B. Slaughter . . . . *G. Howland*
                        Shaw Award Recipient

**and honored
staff and volunteers of
the Bureau.**

PROCEEDS TO BENEFIT
BUREAU OF REHABILITATION, INC.

BUREAU OF
REHABILITATION INC.

May 1, 1986

Ms. Bernice Slaughter

Dear Ms. Slaughter:

    On behalf of our clients, Board, staff and volunteers again
I want to express to you our appreciation for being the recipient
of our 7th G. Howland Shaw award at our awards banquet on April
22nd.

    The evening was such a great success and I know you had a
large part to play in making it so.   You are indeed a special
person in many ways, well deserving of the acclaim you have
received for your contributions at Occoquan specifically and the
field of corrections generally.

                          Sincerely yours,

                          Harry A. Manley
                          Executive Director

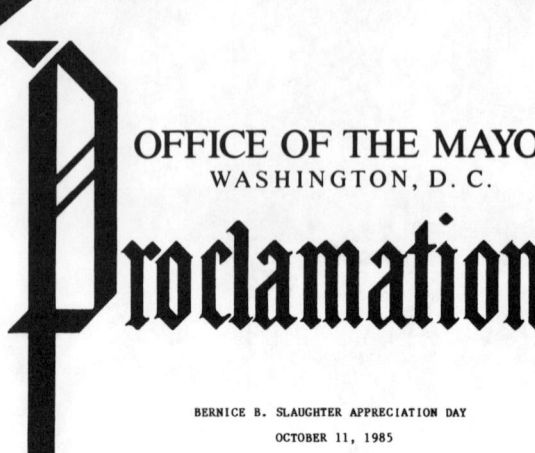

OFFICE OF THE MAYOR
WASHINGTON, D. C.

Proclamation

BERNICE B. SLAUGHTER APPRECIATION DAY

OCTOBER 11, 1985

BY THE MAYOR OF THE DISTRICT OF COLUMBIA

WHEREAS, on Friday, October 11, 1985, a dedication ceremony will be held to present formally the new pews in the restored chapel at the Occoquan Correctional facilities; and

WHEREAS, the efforts of Mrs. Bernice Slaughter provided the cornerstone of the support garnered for the restoration of the Interfaith Chapel, and her dedication to this enterprise has remained unswerving and undaunted; and

WHEREAS, Mrs. Slaughter solicited over twenty-six thousand dollars from the religious and business communities for the restoration of the chapel and eight thousand dollars for the new pews; and

WHEREAS, Mrs. Slaughter's devotion to the tenets of Christianity has enabled her to pursue her goals while maintaining an optimistic outlook and appreciating the universal need for a spiritual foundation to all endeavors; and

WHEREAS, in keeping with the concepts of unconditional love and generosity of spirit, the Interfaith Chapel represents the labor and care of the entire prison community, numerous religious and business leaders, and, above all, the faith of Mrs. Bernice Slaughter:

NOW, THEREFORE, I, THE MAYOR OF THE DISTRICT OF COLUMBIA, do hereby proclaim Friday, October 11, 1985 as **"BERNICE B. SLAUGHTER APPRECIATION DAY"** in the District of Columbia, in grateful recognition of her magnificent gifts of service to our city, and call upon all the residents of Washington, D.C. to join with me in saluting her spiritual vision and thanking all the contributors to this beautiful addition to the Occoquan Correctional facilities.

MARION S. BARRY, JR.
MAYOR

Council of the District of Columbia

Resolution

Councilmember Crawford presents the following Resolution co-sponsored by:

Chairman Clarke   Councilmember Jarvis   Councilmember Kane

Councilmember Mason   Councilmember Ray   Councilmember Rolark

Councilmember Schwartz   Councilmember Shackleton   Councilmember Smith

Councilmember Spaulding   Councilmember Wilson   Councilmember Winter

BERNICE B. SLAUGHTER RECOGNITION RESOLUTION OF 1985

WHEREAS, BERNICE B. SLAUGHTER VOLUNTEERED TO START AN INMATE CHOIR AT THE LORTON CORRECTIONAL COMPLEX IN JANUARY, 1985;

WHEREAS, BERNICE B. SLAUGHTER, UPON SEEING THE DILAPIDATED CONDITION OF THE CHAPEL, RESOLVED THAT THE CHAPEL WOULD BE REBUILT TO MAKE IT A FIT PLACE TO ENHANCE THE SPIRITUAL GROWTH OF INMATES;

WHEREAS, BERNICE B. SLAUGHTER AND HER HUSBAND CONTRIBUTED $3,100 FROM THEIR PERSONAL FUNDS FOR THE WALL MATERIALS FOR THE RENOVATION;

WHEREAS, BERNICE B. SLAUGHTER RAISED AN ADDITIONAL $23,000 FROM MINISTERS, FRIENDS, LOCAL BUSINESSES, AND RELATIVES;

WHEREAS, BERNICE B. SLAUGHTER, THROUGH HER DETERMINATION AND DEDICATION, INSPIRED MANY OF THE INMATES TO CONTRIBUTE THEIR LABOR TO THE PROJECT, SOME WORKING UP TO 16 HOURS A DAY;

WHEREAS, BERNICE B. SLAUGHTER AND HER HUSBAND DROVE 32 MILES TO THE PRISON SEVERAL TIMES A WEEK TO CARRY MATERIALS AND SUPPLIES FOR THE RENOVATION;

WHEREAS, BERNICE B. SLAUGHTER, WHO ALSO SUPERVISED THE WORK ON THE CHAPEL, WAS ABLE TO GUIDE THE PROJECT TO COMPLETION AT NO COST TO THE DISTRICT GOVERNMENT, A PROJECT THAT WOULD HAVE COST $150,000 HAD IT BEEN DONE COMMERCIALLY; AND

WHEREAS, BERNICE B. SLAUGHTER HAS ORGANIZED AND INITIATED A SERIES OF SPIRITUAL ENRICHMENT SERVICES THAT CONSISTENTLY DRAW STANDING ROOM ONLY PARTICIPATION IN THE NEWLY NAMED INTERFAITH CHAPEL.

RESOLVED, BY THE COUNCIL OF THE DISTRICT OF COLUMBIA, THAT THIS RESOLUTION MAY BE SITED AS THE "BERNICE B. SLAUGHTER RECOGNITION RESOLUTION OF 1985".

SEC. 2. THE COUNCIL OF THE DISTRICT OF COLUMBIA RECOGNIZES THE OUTSTANDING DEDICATION AND LEADERSHIP OF BERNICE B. SLAUGHTER IN BRINGING TO FRUITION A PROJECT WHICH WILL CONTINUE TO HAVE A POSITIVE IMPACT ON THE LIVES OF PRISON INMATES FOR YEARS TO COME.

This resolution shall take effect immediately.

_____
CHAIRMAN OF THE COUNCIL

I hereby Certify that this Resolution is true and adopted as stated herein.

Resolution Number: 6-323

OCTOBER 8, 1985

_____
SECRETARY TO THE COUNCIL

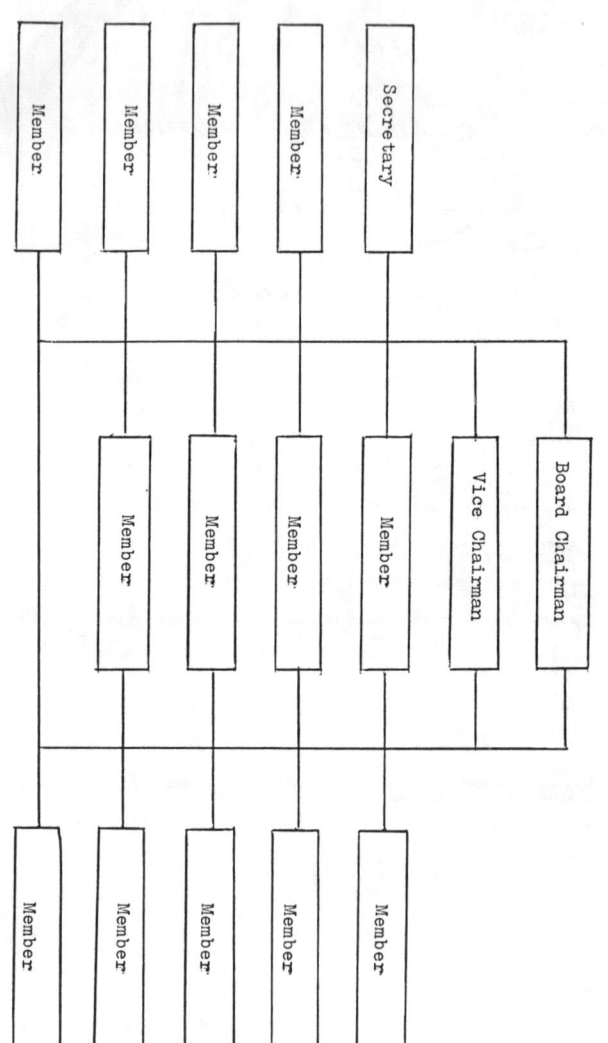

Figure: 19

ORGANIZATIONAL CHART

EVOL PRISON MINISTRY, INCORPORATED

"The Golden Hour"

Dedication of Pews

Celebrating Completion

of

Occoquan 1 and 2
Prison Chapel Project

Friday, October 11, 1985
At 1:30 p. m.

Bernice B. Slaughter
Religious Volunteer
Coordinator, Occoquan Prison
Chapel Project

Figure 21

A Board Member Speaks

The Rev. Herbert A. Schwandt, Board Member
of EVOL Prison Ministry, Inc.

"In the seventeenth chapter of Acts, the apostle Paul and Silas were on the second missionary journey. They came to Thessalonica and proclaimed Jesus as the Christ. This seemed to arouse jealousy and anger and violence on the part of the leaders who instigated a riot and brought them before the authorities saying: 'These men who have turned the world upside down have come here also'. Then, as now, the Gospel is still the power of God unto salvation to all who believe. It is foolishness to men, but to those who believe, it is the power of God unto salvation. In a manner of speaking, you might say, our very title, 'E.V.O.L.', is a witness to that fact. We came in love and to help, but we were seen as a threat. Some have, perhaps, felt that we have come to turn the prison upside down and some have reacted as if that were the case. We accept the fact that some may look at it backwards even as they did with Paul and Silas. We have not come to turn the prison system upside down or society upside down; we who come in the name of the Christ have come to turn it right side up! Just as our title designates, E.V.O.L. is *LOVE*!"

Figure 22

An Ex-offender Speaks

> *". . . there's a reason to life!*
> *We can lift ourselves out of ignorance,*
> *we can find ourselves as creatures of*
> *excellence and intelligence and skill.*
> *We can be free! We can learn to fly!"*
>
> *(Jonathan Livingston Seagull,*
> *Richard Bach)*

The first thing one must do each morning, especially if he is a prisoner at Occoquan, is to discover a reason to live. The idea that one is indeed alive, in general, and the quality of that life in particular, seems to get lost in bureaucratic apathy and sociological ignorance. The idea that anti-social habits can only be displaced by socially acceptable education has been lost in a political abyss of bickering and the struggle between liberalism and the conservative "new" right. The result is present-day Occoquan where a myriad of inmates awaken every morning to face another unfinited day of moral decadence. They see old broken down buildings, overcrowding, limited toileting facilities, poor health and educational services, no rehabilitative programs and no incentive to become productive. A good and socially productive life is expected to rise up by way of spontaneous generation. A reason to live is displaced by the mere necessity to exist.

Occoquan is a festering sore on the Nation's Capital's criminal justice system. It is a boil which will break open one day soon, emptying all of its ugliness into the lives of society. Occoquan is no timeless vaccination against Washington's crime problems. Rather, like polio, a few criminals are placed in temporary docility to sleep for a while and grow strong, to later rise up in the city's streets much stronger, with much greater crippling potential. A relatively minor eruption already occurred recently when fire, smoke, and mace rose in a magic mist over the bricks and barbed wire barriers of Occoquan. It was an eruption caused by about fifty men and the system punished nine hundred and fifty spreading them all over the country. It was an eruption where an unskilled officer shot one nineteen-year-old man (who did not participate in the disturbance) in the face and killed him while he lay sleeping on the ground in an act of nonselective retaliation. Occoquan is an explosion which may not happen today, but it is an explosion that must rise out of the timeless truths of evil.

"Men at Occoquan have it good," some say. "They can stay up and watch cable television all night if they wish." The truth is that the administration permits the television sets to stay on because they have nothing else to do with all of the men they keep. There are *less than one hundred and fifty jobs for over thirteen hundred men.* There is a school that graduated only seven of six hundred men in June, 1986, a school always short on paper, pencils, books, teachers and *education.* There are, therefore, the television sets which become mother, father, lover, teacher and counselor to hundreds of men with problems.

Occoquan is a "melting pot" of evil. It does not use diagnostic classification for most residents; therefore, mental illness and other problems are not discovered until it is too late. One teacher was beaten and nearly raped by a man who has an extensive history of mental illness and inappropriate sexual behavior. He had been placed in lock-up two weeks earlier for masturbating in a classroom. He was neither counseled nor given any other help. The teacher, one of Occoquan's few good instructors, was transferred. Men who are trying are mixed with men who are not yet ready to try. Men who are old and sick are mixed with men who are barely men at all. One never knows who or what he will meet from one moment to the next.

"I do not come with timeless truths
My consciousness is not illuminated with ultimate radiances.
Nevertheless, in complete composure, I think it would be
        good if certain things were said.

These things I am going to say, not shout.
For it is a long time since shouting has gone
        out of my life. So very long . . .

. . . From all sides dozens and hundreds of pages
        assail me . . . But a single line would be enough.
Supply a single answer and the *prison* problem would
        be stripped of all of its importance.

        What does man want?"

                                        (*Black Skin, White Masks*
                                        by Frantz Fanon)

It is obvious that since man learned to make and obey laws, he also learns to break them. Learning is the result of good education; therefore, man is what he has learned to become. He will be what he learns to be. At Occoquan, that which most men *learn to be* will turn the stomachs of most people who have never gone there. At Occoquan, man learns to exist out of necessity. He is guided by a natural will to survive, and survival is all most men can hope to accomplish.

Correctional officers are bored and discontented since one of the greatest of their responsibilities is to learn to turn keys. Dealing with people is learned along the way or not at all at the expense of the inmates and other officers. Many are as much prisoners as the inmates.

The answer is simple. Open the doors to the public. Let the people deal with people who need help. There must be contact with society now when it can help. To drop men into society after years of Occoquan is a shock that neither may absorb. The answer is simple: inmates are only human. Like you, they are what they have learned. They become what they learn—what you teach.

Stop being blinded to Occoquan, *BEFORE* it devours you, and teach them well.

"I am an invisible man. No, I am not a spook like those who haunted Edgar Allan Poe; nor am I one of your Hollywood-movie ectoplasms. I am a man of substance, of flesh and bone, fiber and liquids—and I might even be said to possess a mind. I am invisible, understand, simply because people refuse to see me."

(*Invisible Man*, by Ralph Ellison)

Ex-offender Theodore Hawkins
Occoquan Facility

BERNICE

by
James N. Slaughter, Jr.

Figure 23

SHE MAKES A DIFFERENCE

A Note About the Caring Character . . .

Bernice Slaughter is an experience. One would have to have been closely associated with her over a long period of years to be able to even begin to extrapolate from this book any true sense of the extent of her accomplishment at Occoquan. This is equally true of countless other seemingly impossible feats that she has successfully orchestrated.

The reader may need to be reminded that it was not just luck that Mrs. Slaughter was able to secure the cooperation of so many diverse individuals and groups in making her dream a reality. Further, it stops somewhere short of truth to think that all who helped did so to be part of a great humanitarian effort. This, yes, but the greater part of the motivation derived from the inevitable fulfillment of this Bible-based assurance: "Cast your bread upon the waters: for thou shalt find it after many days . . ."

It seems no exaggeration to this admirer of Bernice Slaughter to say that anyone who knows her (and many who don't) has at one time or another benefitted by her talent, her wide range of skills and her unselfishness in sharing these with all who stand in need of them. It is only in this light that one can get a feel for the kind of reciprocity on the part of Mrs. Slaughter's widespread circle of friends and acquaintances that enabled her to present first a piano, then an organ, then hymnals, then pews and a pulpit and finally, a completely renovated chapel.

Mrs. Slaughter's work reminds us of the job of building a chapel by Mr. Smith and the German nuns in William Barrett's novel, *The Lillies of the Field*. Mr. Smith, unlike Mrs. Slaughter, wants no part of such a Herculean task. Who can build a chapel with no money, no workers, no materials?

> *"If you think that I'm building that, you're out of your mind," he said. "I'm one man. I aint no contrtactor with a crew. I don't need all that work, neither."* To which the head nun , not at all daunted, replies, *"Ve are vimen. Ve build it."* The chapel was, indeed built. The concluding lines of the story? **"There is no chapel like it anywhere."**

Dr. Doris Gladden Pointer
Lanham, Maryland

Figure 24

The Volunteer Speaks

It is gratifying to witness the success of many inmates, who as a result of their acceptance of the aid, compassion and comfort afforded by the community, have come to function creditably in society.

One of the greatest challenges I have ever faced is to relieve the human suffering experienced at Occoquan. Yes, it's been difficult, but I was an outsider having no authority, no right to be there and was at the mercy of those in authority. I understood and respected the responsibility the administration has for the prison. However, I believe that if I am about rebuilding lives, the spiritual dimension is one opportunity on which I cannot close the door. In the words of Edgar A. Guest, " Love has the patience to endure the faults it sees but cannot cure."

—Bernice B. Slaughter

Figure 25

Commentary

There has been little or no reason to doubt that this correctional system produces inmate recidivism. Not only has this been revealed by some of the staff members of various levels and by some of the correctional officers, but it is a conclusion arrived at on the strength of extensive exposure to the operation of the system and the familiarity with it.

I wonder, why is it that the guardian of the district's prisoners would be so interested in assuring their continuous confinement? What possible benefit could be derived from the ex-offenders' inability to function productively and legitimately in society? Is there any logical rationale for the *institutionalization* of inmates? Why must they be so savagely deprived of even a semblance of humane treatment? Is it that they all deserve the kind of total alienation from civilized behavior which I have so painfully observed? Is it necessary that narcotics would be more plentiful, more readily available in the prison cell than on the street corner as noted in an inmates letter appearing in chapter eleven, "BLURBS FROM INMATES?" And, why should a prison VOLUNTEER, devoted only to the well-being and rehabilitation of the inmate, seemingly become the object of such vile rejection enormously dispensed? The answer, I have discovered is lodged in the reality that this system is really *"big business."* The inmates have tried to help me understand this. It is motivated solely by a frantic, paranoid determination to perpetuate itself. "Without the constant influx of repeat offenders," several correctional officers infer, "job security would be threatened." And so, this correctional corporation does masterfully continue a *systematic dehumanization* of many of those languishing there at Occoquan.

The effort, however, was to offer an *alternative.* Into the midst of this depository of human carnage did we introduce to them someone who cared whether they lived or died, and loved them inspite of what they had done and despite what they had become. The inmates often relate to Bernice their appreciation of her *non-judgmental* attitude toward them. "She only wants us to be the best we can be, to become productive citizens and in the process she had given everything possible, *FOR US!* We know that she loves us and wants nothing in return but our success," remarked an inmate. Many others chorused their assent.

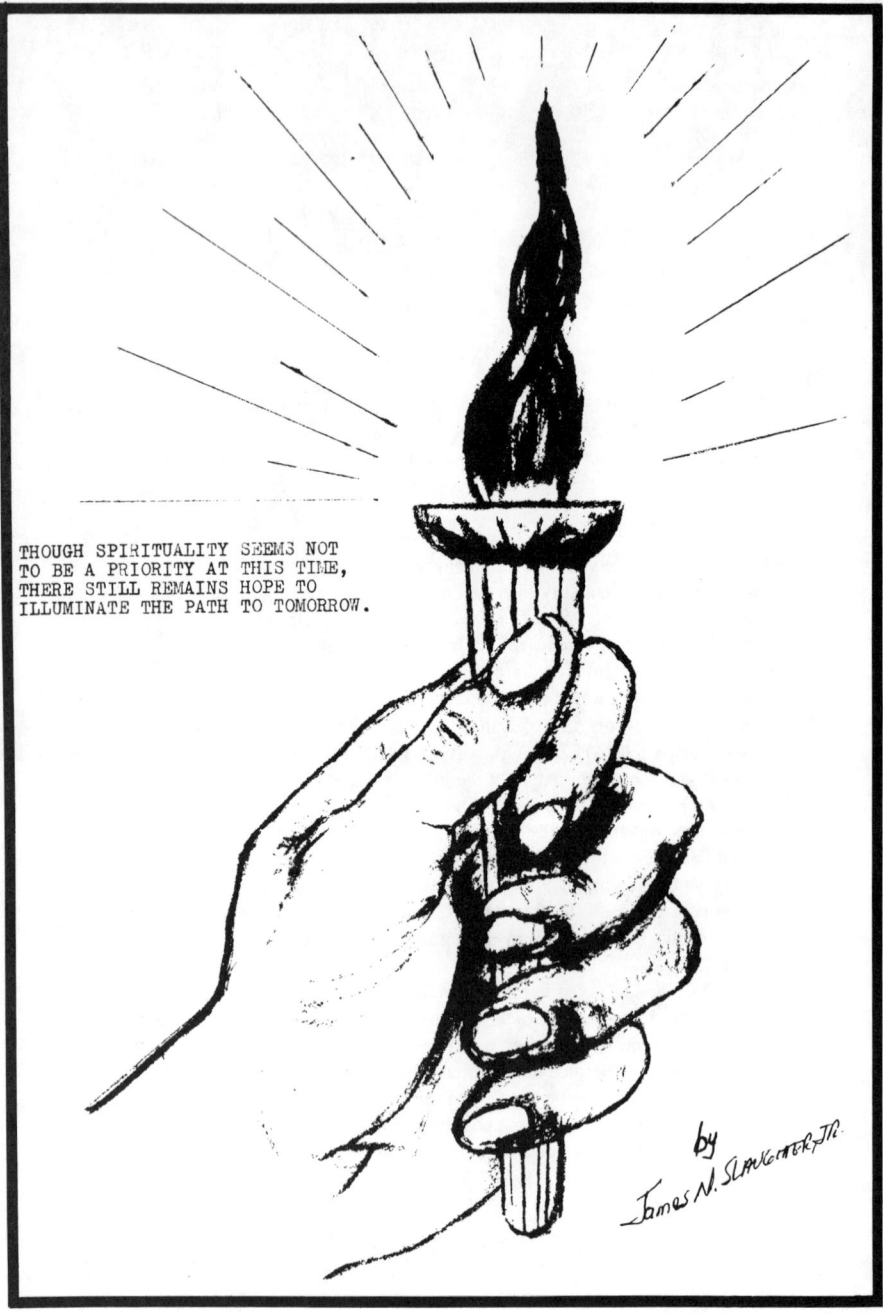

THOUGH SPIRITUALITY SEEMS NOT
TO BE A PRIORITY AT THIS TIME,
THERE STILL REMAINS HOPE TO
ILLUMINATE THE PATH TO TOMORROW.

by
James N. Slaughter, JR.

She has jeopardized her life for the inmates there; and so there has developed a special kind of maternal relationship with them. Some staff explained,

"You see, Mrs, Slaughter brought a new dimension into the penal system. Many in the system fail to realize that a District of Columbia prisoner identification number (D. C. Number) is easy to come by. Some are jealous out of ignorance. When the inmates hear that Mrs. Slaughter is coming, showers are quickly utilized; shirt tails are carefully tucked in; mattress-pressed trousers are worn; the grooming in general is conspicuously improved." Respect invites respect.

"When Mrs. Slaughter calls for you, man, you are honored . . . what can I do to get her attention?" says an inmate. Seemingly the level of respect allows some officers to feel strong resentment. Unfortunately, too many of them do not enjoy similar regard. "It is heart breaking to witness the humiliation and frustration that is inflicted upon Bernice. All we can do is look upon the situation with weeping eyes," says an officer. "It's like paying a price for a sacrifice. Isn't that a part of life?" Bernice conjectured.

With some self-reproach another staff member declared: "We are reluctant to show Bernice a visible kind of respect because of possible reprisal against us. While some don't like her, they respect her because *she has made a difference* . . . she's fulfilling her mission. She bore many a cross to help an inmate. Not only did she ease the suffering for all, but she endured plenty that the inmates might be saved."

While striving to offer much in terms of interpersonal relationships, Bernice aspires to people who exhibit a degree of self-awareness, honesty, trustworthiness, a profound belief in their self-worth and a mission in life. She praises the inmates for their honesty and trustworthiness which is somewhat more than can be said for some people in the free society.

The Author